MW00473841

BETWEEN THE DEVIL AND THE SEA

BETWEEN THE

Illustrations by Don Miller

New York and London

DEVIL AND THE SEA

The Life of
James Forten

By Brenda A. Johnston

HBJ Harcourt Brace Jovanovich

Mar '75

Text copyright © 1974 by Brenda A. Johnston
Illustrations copyright © 1974 by Harcourt Brace Jovanovich, Inc.

Printed in the United States of America

First edition

B C D E F G H I J K

Library of Congress Cataloging in Publication Data

Johnston, Brenda A.
Between the devil and the sea.

SUMMARY: A biography of the free black man who became a wealthy
Philadelphia sailmaker and active abolitionist.
Bibliography: p.
1. Forten, James—Juvenile literature. [1. Forten, James.
2. Slavery in the United States—Anti-slavery movements.
3. Negroes—Biography] I. Miller, Don, 1923–   illus. II. Title.
E185.97.F717J64   322.4'4'0924 [B] [92]   74–5603
ISBN 0-15-206965-8

To my sister, Terri,
my first and most loyal fan

Contents

BETWEEN THE DEVIL AND THE SEA

1

Father and Son

JAMES awakened to the aroma of baking biscuits mingling with the odor of onion-fried potatoes and scrapple. He lay quietly, savoring the contentment of his warm bed, his mother's busy sounds, and the delicious smells that filled the house. A moment later, however, he remembered the importance of today. In excitement he bounded from the warm bed to the cold floor, fearful that his father might forget or change his mind. He had told James that he would take him to work with him today, but James knew that if he did not hurry with his chores, his mother might talk his father into making him go to school instead.

He quickly made his bed, dressed, and then ran out to the backyard to bring in the firewood for the day. He stacked it in neat piles on the porch, then hurriedly washed his face and, running into the kitchen, slid into his chair, his face still half wet.

"Mother, please hurry," he said impatiently.

She didn't answer, but deposited his plate in front of him, then stood back studying him for a moment. She dried his face with the hem of her apron.

11

James started eating but after a moment complained, "Oh, Mother, you gave me too much. I don't have time to finish."

"Well, you had better eat it," she said, "or stay home."

James's father smiled. "Don't eat so fast, James. We have plenty of time. And you'd best clean your plate, too, because we don't eat again until twelve o'clock."

James slowed down and somehow managed to clean his plate just as his sister, Abigail, came into the kitchen.

"Well, good morning," James said importantly, "and how are you?"

"Shut up," she replied.

"If Fred and Larry come by," James went on, "just tell them that I went to work today." He picked up his lunch from the table.

Abigail's eyes filled with tears. "Girls can't do anything. James gets to go to school. James gets to go to work. I can't do anything."

Her father picked her up and swung her high above his head. "You know something?" he said. "I'm going to bring you back something real nice. O.K.?" Abigail had to laugh.

Holding his father's hand and walking in the darkness and quiet of the early morning, James felt proud and happy. He loved his father so much. He was a tall, medium-brown man with a soft voice and laughing eyes. He took pride in everything he did and was known along the wharves of Philadelphia as a hard worker. He was a sailmaker in the sail loft of Mr. Robert Bridges. Two of the young apprentices in the loft were ill, so Thomas Forten had volunteered James's services to Mr. Bridges.

As soon as they entered the shop, James began to thread

the needles. His father showed him how to make the twine the exact length of the sewer's arm so that it wouldn't dangle or be in his way. He showed him how to wax the twine so it would hold for the best sails in all Philadelphia. That was the hardest part of the job. James had to rub the wax ball very carefully over the long yards of twine. He worked until his arms ached and his fingers were stiff. Still he would not stop, for he wanted his father to be proud of him. Finally, Mr. Bridges noticed James hunching and unhunching his shoulders and called him over.

"James," he said, "you have worked as hard today as a man. We could use you around here. Can you come back tomorrow?"

James couldn't believe it. Most of the time you had to be at least fourteen to be able to work, and here he was just nine years old and offered a job already. He turned his eager eyes to his father, but Mr. Forten was already shaking his head. He wanted James to be a sailmaker someday, but not now. Now he was a child.

"I'm sorry, Mr. Bridges, but James has to go to school tomorrow," his father said.

"School?" Mr. Bridges was shocked. He had no idea that Thomas Forten was sending James to school. There was only one private school for black children in all Philadelphia. Reaching into his pocket, Mr. Bridges pulled out a shilling and handed it to James. "Someday," he said with a laugh, "you'll have my job, James."

James's father took his hand. They walked back along the waterfront of the Delaware River much slower than they had walked this morning, for now James was very tired. As he looked at the red sun sinking into the dark gray river, he realized that the whole day was over and he didn't get to do his lessons for tomorrow or play even one

game of marbles with his friends. His shoulders felt numb and his eyes were heavy. He didn't think that he liked working very much after all.

His father must have read his mind, for he squeezed James's hand and said, "You look so much like your grandfather. You worked for a shilling today. Father worked as a slave all day for nothing; then he would turn around and work all night for a half-shilling. Day and night he worked until he could buy his own freedom and your grandma's, too." His voice was sad but proud. He paused for a moment and then went on softly, as if he were no longer aware of James. "But I'm free, and, my son, you will never be a slave." Sighing, he continued more cheerfully. "But work is for a man. Tomorrow you go to school. Tomorrow you play with your friends. You'll be a man soon enough."

2
Tragedy

AFTER his experience working, James was glad to return to the routine of school and play. He, Larry Williams, and Fred Saunders were inseparable, but James was the undisputed leader of the trio. He was also the marble champion of the neighborhood, and the schoolmaster, Mr. Benezet, said that his handwriting was the best in the class.

In 1776 Philadelphia was an exciting city to live in for ten-year-old James. He and his friends would walk along the docks and watch the new ships built by the Continental Army.

"What does that say?" James demanded of his friends, knowing that they could not read. He was pointing to the motto painted on one of the ships.

When they didn't answer, he told them, "It says, 'Don't Tread on Me.'"

"I knew that one word was 'on,'" said Larry.

"You should know more than that by now," said James. "You've seen some of those words a thousand times."

"I can copy any letter," bragged Fred, "but I can't read words."

16

"Just copy the words when you know what they spell," said James. "That way you can learn to read and write."

Their conversation was suddenly interrupted by the sound of the State House bell tolling. It was rung only in emergencies. The boys ran to the State House yard, where many people were already gathered. A man stood on a platform and read a very legal-sounding document. James couldn't understand the wording, but from the shouting and talk afterward, he knew that the colonies would no longer be ruled by Great Britain. The boys caught the excitement of the crowd and sang and danced with them on the State House lawn.

When his father got home that night, James told him that he had been at the State House and heard the Declaration of Independence.

"Father," he asked, "why do white people have to be free? Aren't they free already?"

His father smiled his slow smile and said, "In a way they are free, but their country is not free."

"When they free the country," asked James, "does that mean that all the people of the country are then free?"

"Yes, it does," answered his father.

"You mean slavery will be over, Father?" said James, jumping up in excitement.

"Wait a minute, James," replied his father. "No, that's not what I mean. Slavery probably will not be over."

"What?" asked James angrily. "Why not! This is our country too."

"You're free," said his father. "You don't ever have to worry about being a slave. Your grandfather saw to that."

"But what about all the other slaves, Father?" said James.

Mr. Forten was silent for a moment. "Slavery will end eventually, James. Maybe in your own lifetime, but don't

17

think that all slaves are ready to be free and to take care of themselves. Some could be free right now if they wanted to work for it."

"But why does each black person have to work for his own freedom and all the white people in the country decide to be free at the same time?" James's voice was bitter.

"It's not that simple, James," his father replied. "You're much too young to be worrying about things like that. Wait until you finish school at least." He patted James's shoulder. "You'll be so smart then that maybe you'll have the answer."

The next day after school a very troubled James asked Mr. Benezet about freeing the slaves.

"Why is the Declaration of Independence we heard yesterday just to free white people?"

"Well," said Mr. Benezet slowly, "it's different for the white man and the black man. This country belongs to the white man."

"But why?" interrupted James.

"Well," he started again, this time more slowly than before. "The white men founded the country. They control it with money, education, and everything else it takes to make a country. This is the white man's culture and not the black man's, so that puts the blacks at a disadvantage."

"Where is our country, then, if not here?" asked James. "Africa?"

"No," said Mr. Benezet quickly. "And England is not my home, although it was the home of my ancestors. The poor slaves are ignorant and without organization, my lad, but they are men. When they adapt to this society, they will someday stand up and claim their independence the same way as these countrymen have declared theirs." He cleared his throat, and his voice became more solemn. "But don't think that it is easy, James. It takes more than just one piece of paper to free a man or a country. There will be bloodshed and treason and hate before freedom is really attained."

As he talked, he walked to the window, his hands locked behind his back. He wanted very much to say something encouraging to James. Now he understood why white people were so against education for the blacks, who might then realize the reason for and solution to their plight. Standing there in silence, wondering what to say next, he was surprised to see Abigail, James's sister, running up the walk. She was crying.

"Abigail," said Mr. Benezet, opening the door. "What is wrong?"

Abigail turned her tiny tear-streaked face to James and cried, "Oh, James, come quickly. It's Father. He was fastening sails and he fell into the river."

James's heart froze in terror. "Oh no," he cried, running from the house and leaving Abigail and Mr. Benezet to follow behind. He ran down to the wharves, where a sheet-covered body lay. He knew instinctively that it was his father. He ran up to the body and would have removed the sheet, but Mr. Bridges caught him up in his arms.

"No, James," he said softly. "It's too late."

Vaguely, James heard Abigail screaming in the background.

Mr. Benezet and Mr. Bridges led the two children home. Abigail was sobbing wildly, but James, struck dumb with grief, could not cry. Their mother stood at the door with a group of her friends. Without saying a word, she took their hands and led them alone into the house. Sitting between them on the sofa, she rocked them gently until they fell asleep.

Sometime very late that night, James awakened on the sofa, forgetting for a moment why he was so sad. Then he remembered his father. In the dark quiet of the house, he could hear his mother sobbing in her room. James crept quietly from the house, closing the door behind him. He ran down to the dark river, where he had spent so many happy days with his father. He almost expected to see the body still lying on the dock, but there was nothing to be seen—only the white, grasping waves on the black river. The tears came at last, and a very small boy became a man.

3
The Rescue

James awakened from a restless sleep. He had been cold all night. Anxious to build up the fire, he jumped from the bed, his teeth chattering, and dressed hurriedly. Quickly he brought in piles of driftwood so he could save the logs. It was almost impossible to transport cut logs for firewood now that the British navy guarded the ports. While James was building up the fire, his mother came in, clutching her ragged shawl close to her shoulders.

"James," she said, knowing that he would soon be gone for the day, "please don't leave until you eat."

"Oh, Mother," he replied impatiently, "I don't have time to eat. I've got to gather more wood before I go to work."

She set the pot of water on the stove as if she hadn't heard him and, opening the cupboard, took out the cornmeal. James's heart sank. If there was one thing that he did not want to see this morning, it was cornmeal mush. They had had it for dinner the night before. His job at the store paid little, and James knew how carefully his mother spent the money. Still he missed her good cooking of earlier days.

"James"—his mother began again—"I want you to come

home when the store closes. Now you know how dangerous it is for you to be running around since that British drummer boy, God bless his soul, was killed."

"Mother," said James in exasperation, "you know that was in a rock battle two years ago. I wasn't even throwing. Besides, I'm too big to play that game now. I'm almost fifteen. Why can't you let me join the navy?"

"James, don't start arguing with Mother about that again this morning," put in Abigail as she clomped into the kitchen, making an extraordinary amount of noise, even for her.

"What in the world do you have on?" asked James, looking at her feet.

At his surprised look, she said sullenly, "Yes, they're father's shoes. It's cold outside and one of mine's busted."

"You're so silly," said James angrily. Seeing his father's shoes brought memories of a better day flooding back to his mind. It had been five years now since his father had drowned, but sometimes it seemed like only yesterday.

His mother set the hot cornmeal mush down in front of James. The smell of it made him sick with disgust. His mother apparently didn't notice his distaste, for she and Abigail began eating.

"Read this to me," she said, placing a newspaper in front of him. James looked at it and quickly read it to himself. It was an announcement that all slaves fighting for the British were forever free and that colored soldiers could be trained for any occupation they wished in the British army.

"I can't," said James deliberately.

"You can't what?" asked his mother, a look of fright on her face.

"I can't read it," he answered, tossing the newspaper back to the table. He knew this would upset his mother, for every so often she would ask him if he could still read. He had never gone back to school after his father died. He shoved his chair back suddenly, leaving his untouched mush. Reading the article made him angry. American slogans of freedom like "Give me liberty or give me death" were his mottos, too. He despised the British and hated the traitors, slave or free, who joined their ranks. He would rather be like Crispus Attucks of the Boston Massacre, an escaped slave who had died fighting the British. If only his mother would listen.

His lips tight with anger, he stormed out the door. He took his sled and headed toward the sail loft before going to collect firewood. James had stopped there daily since his father's death. He kept the floor shining clean and as smooth as glass. Then he would wait around to see if Mr. Bridges needed anything. Five years ago, Mr. Bridges had allowed James to run errands because he sensed the boy's need to be reminded of his father. As time went on, however, James began doing all types of jobs for Mr. Bridges, from waxing the twine to filling in for the apprentices when they were out. Sometimes Mr. Bridges would look up from cutting the canvas into sails and realize that James must have been watching him for hours. He believed that James was eager to do even that job, which was reserved for only the most skilled of sailmakers. More and more, without realizing it, everyone at the loft expected James to help out during the day. Sometimes Mr. Bridges paid him a shilling, but most of the time he gave him nothing.

This morning, as James paused outside to look at the freezing Delaware, he noticed young Thomas Willig maneuvering a small boat on the river. James watched for a moment, wondering why he was out there all alone. His father was Thomas Willig, Sr., who owned nearly all the warehouses along the Delaware, including the one where Mr. Bridges's loft was located. James and Thomas were the same age, and when they were quite young, they had sometimes played together while waiting for their fathers.

As James turned to go, he heard a scream. Thomas's boat had capsized and the boy sank out of sight for a moment, then surfaced again, struggling wildly. Because his own father had drowned, James had trained himself to be a powerful swimmer, and now he threw off his coat and plunged into the water. He grabbed the struggling boy by his hair and started for shore. Although they were just a short distance from land, the icy water penetrated James's body and sucked his strength so that only by great effort was he able to pull himself and the half-drowned Thomas to shore. He covered Thomas with his own coat and then ran, gasping, up the steps calling for Mr. Bridges. In the warm sail loft Thomas was soon revived, and in the excitement James slipped away.

He arrived home coatless, shivering, and still half damp, his sled empty. His mother cried out when she saw him. While he tried to tell her what had happened, she built the fire up to a roaring blaze and began helping him out of his wet clothes. She piled all the blankets in the house on him, and from somewhere in the empty kitchen she found some tea. Finally, the hot tea and blazing fire lulled him into a contented sleep.

He was awakened hours later by the sound of voices. His mother was talking to Mr. Bridges and Mr. Willig. He could hear her saying over and over again, "Thank you. Thank you. God bless you." She closed the door behind them and walked over to James. Her hand felt cool on his face. When she saw that he was awake, she dropped a small bag down on his chest. James opened it to see that it contained one hundred dollars in silver coins.

"From Thomas Willig," said his mother, answering his unspoken question. "He's grateful to you and I'm very proud myself."

James fingered the money gingerly. He had never seen so much at one time. His mother suddenly laid a Bible on his chest.

"Read this to me," she commanded. James struggled to a sitting position and started reading aloud from the Bible. Just as abruptly his mother took it. "So you can still read," she said accusingly. "Abigail told me that you probably could. See that you read it to me every night from now on." With a sigh of relief, she disappeared into the kitchen. A moment later she came back, carrying a bowl of hot cornmeal mush. James couldn't think of anything he wanted more.

4

The *Royal Lewis*

T HERE was excitement along the harbor, and James joined the crowds watching the *Royal Lewis,* Philadelphia's own privateer, bringing its captured British vessel into port. Since Philadelphia was the capital of the new nation, James witnessed many auctions of captured British cargo at the wharves and marveled at the proceeds that the captain and the crew shared as a reward. The privateers were not part of the navy, but American pirate ships whose mission was to stop the British merchant ships. Their reward was patriotic glory, the wealthy cargo from the captured ships, and a small monthly allotment as well.

James wanted to join the privateer crew more than anything else in the world, but he had already learned that it was useless to plead with his mother. As he walked home from the docks, he passed the London Coffee House, where he met his friends Larry and Fred standing outside.

"Guess what?" They greeted him in excitement.

"What?" asked James coolly, careful not to betray his curiosity.

"Guess who got signed up for the *Royal Lewis*'s next trip?"

James was interested. "Not you, I know," he said, hoping with all his heart that they were not going before he could.

"Daniel Brewton," they answered him. Daniel was one of their white friends.

"I'm going to sign up, too," said James decisively.

"You're too young," said Fred.

"Daniel and I are the same age almost," said James.

"Your mother'll kill you," declared Larry. "Besides, we already tried."

James left them standing there while he approached a man sitting at a table taking down names. He stood before the man and cleared his throat.

The man looked at him inquiringly for a moment, then asked sharply, "How old are you?"

"Sixteen," said James, thinking fast. He was already nearly six feet tall and walked with a slow, self-confident gait. Black bushy eyebrows framed a lean creamed-coffee face and gave him the appearance of a scowl until one of his slow smiles broke through, lit his eyes, and showed two rows of perfect white teeth. His smiles were rare though, and most of the time his face was expressionless. He had acquired the habit of gazing unfalteringly into a person's eyes while talking, but taking care that none of his own feelings were ever reflected in his dark eyes. He now fixed his gaze on the man and waited.

The man finally shrugged his shoulders and said, "Oh, well. You're on. What's your name?"

"James Forten," he answered quickly, already wondering what he was going to tell his mother.

The man's voice broke through his thoughts. "We sail in three days, James. See you then."

He walked back to his friends and with disdain in every word said, "Well, boys, the *Royal Lewis* and *I* sail in three days."

They were astonished. "How?" they asked. "What did you say?"

James laughed at their dismay and patted their heads.

"I think," he said, "that you two are just a little too short." He started for home.

In spite of his apprehension about telling his mother the bad news, James was humming with joy when he reached home. His spirits were so high that even Abigail and his mother caught his mood. James put off telling his mother until he had read to her from the Bible that evening. But as he closed the book, he looked at her and started.

"Mother, can I join the crew of the *Royal Lewis?*"

She didn't answer but just returned his direct look. For a panicky moment, he wondered if someone had already told her what he had done. She acted as if she knew.

"They are taking twenty black sailors with them, Mother," he finally said.

She still would not answer. James wildly thought that either she was a mind reader or she had talked to Larry's mother.

"I'm one of the twenty," he said at last, shamefacedly.

His mother folded her arms and shook her head but did not say anything. It was the only time James had ever defied her. Now he felt sorry.

"Is it all right?" he asked, his voice pleading.

"You did what you wanted to do already, didn't you?" She sounded tired.

"Oh, I'll never get a job in the sail loft so long as the war lasts," said James. "Business keeps getting slower and slower. This way I'll get a chance to do lots of things.

Travel. Defend my country." His eyes sparkled in excitement, and he suddenly laughed aloud.

"Oh, Mother," he exclaimed, "I've always wanted to ride in a ship and see the sails from the other side."

"But, James," she said, her voice almost breaking, "it's so dangerous."

"Not for our ship," said James, "the *Royal Lewis*, commanded by Captain Decatur—King of the Sea."

"Promise me," his mother said, finally relenting, "that you will read your Bible every night. You'll never know how much your father wanted you to be able to read."

"I promise," said James. "Only, Mother, no one can forget how to read. It's like forgetting how to walk."

Three days later James went down to the docks, taking only the clothes he wore on his back, his mother's Bible, and a bag of marbles. On the way he stopped by the sail loft to say good-bye. He was surprised that Mr. Bridges was more emotional about his leaving than his mother had been. They walked to the ship together, and Mr. Bridges stood on shore while James boarded the *Royal Lewis* and stood there waving as the ship weighed anchor and moved out to the open sea. His mother had stayed home and had waved good-bye to James from the door as if he were leaving, as always, only for the day.

5

Winning and Losing

POWDER BOY on the *Royal Lewis* was the lowest and dirtiest of jobs, and James soon realized that it consisted of more than just preparing for battle. He was often called to serve meals, act as cabin boy, and do whatever else no one in particular was assigned to do. James hid his resentment behind an expressionless face and slow smile and tried especially to make himself useful to Captain Decatur. He stood by ready to serve the captain's meals, to clear the table, or to clean the captain's quarters and was soon recognized as being reserved for the service of the captain. As a result, he escaped some of the dirtier jobs.

He was eager for his first battle, and it seemed forever until the day that the cry came from the ship's lookout that the British ship *Activist* had been spotted. The quiet *Royal Lewis* became a whirl of activity as the regular privateers, in a disciplined manner, began running to their respective posts and shouting out orders. James's head was spinning. He had forgotten all he had learned. He didn't know where to start.

"James Forten," a voice called out impatiently, sounding as if it had called him many times before. "Over here!"

James ran over to the gun crew and stood in position near the powder and balls and waited, hoping that no one would notice his trembling. The *Royal Lewis* came remarkably close to the other ship, it seemed, before the voice of the British captain broke the silence.

"This is His Majesty's frigate *Activist*," he called. "What ship is that?"

Captain Decatur's answer was to signal his men to attack. Almost immediately there was a deafening roar followed by a flash of fire from the cannon, and the deck shook under James's feet. The smell of smoke filled the air and blinded him, making him cough and sneeze. He was so frightened that he froze until a sharp nudge on his shoulder reminded him of his job. By blind instinct, he began passing the powder and cannonballs to the loader, who forced them down the muzzle with a ramrod.

Now that the battle was really on, James could see the extreme danger of his job as powder boy. When the ammunition was low, James had to run below deck to the magazine for more powder and cannonballs. He would then have to run back to his post, shielding the explosive powder from the flying sparks, which could ignite an explosion fatal to him. All around him the sparks flew, forcing him to keep moving, although he had to step over the bodies of wounded, groaning men who cried out to him for help. The battle seemed to last an eternity, and both ships appeared to be utterly destroyed. The two ships were so close now that the crew from the *Royal Lewis* began jumping over to the deck of the *Activist* to continue the battle in man-to-man combat. James, however, stayed at his post, passing powder and balls until his arms felt like rubber. The battle finally took an upward

swing when the *Activist* began burning in several places and the captain was seriously wounded. Soon the British flag was lowered in surrender, and the long battle had ended at last.

The *Activist* did not have the rich cargo that James and all the crew of the *Royal Lewis* had hoped for. As James looked around at the mangled ships and the wounded and dead men on both vessels, he wondered if it had been worth it. However, it was just the first of several battles for James, and some of the later ones brought important prisoners or goods that could be exchanged for large amounts of money. But too soon their luck changed.

One day, about three months after that first battle, as the *Royal Lewis* approached a British warship called the *Amphyon,* the lookout suddenly spotted two more British vessels in the distance. Realizing the impossibility of fighting three ships at one time, the *Royal Lewis* decided to make a run for it, but the British took up the chase. Before long, they were close enough to begin firing. At the first shot, Captain Decatur immediately gave orders to strike colors. The American flag fluttered down in surrender.

It was then that James went into a complete panic. He wanted to run and scream. He knew that black sailors were never kept for prisoner exchanges but were sold into slavery in the West Indies as part of the cargo. Running below to his bunk, he had just enough time to snatch up his blanket, Bible, and marbles before he was ordered on deck by one of the British officers. The crew of the *Royal Lewis* was divided into three groups and sent to the three British ships. James was with the group taken by the *Amphyon.* As the prisoners filed past the captain, James was stopped and the captain asked sharply, "What's in that bag, boy?"

"What bag?" said James in confusion, looking down. His marbles in a small cloth sack dangled from his wrist.

"How old are you?" demanded the captain.

"Fifteen," answered James quickly, forgetting his former lie.

"I said, 'What's in that bag?' " the captain demanded again.

"Marbles," James answered, feeling very embarrassed and childish. He didn't know now what had made him bring them.

"What's your name?" asked the captain.

James figured this was the end for him. The captain probably already had a prospective buyer in mind. He stood tall and answered without faltering, "My name is James Forten."

The captain smiled and waved him on. A few hours later, while James sat with the other prisoners, a British youth with rosy cheeks, straight brown hair, and a pouting mouth approached him.

"Are you James Forten, the powder boy from the *Royal Lewis?*" he asked.

James nodded.

"I am Willie Beasley, the son of Sir John, the captain of the *Amphyon*," he said with a heavy British accent. "My father tells me that you brought a bag of marbles on board. I'm a champion. Would you like to play a game?"

James took out his marbles with great pride now and followed Willie on deck. They placed the marbles in a group on the floor between them. At first they played seriously and silently, but soon, in boyish glee, they were laughing and teasing. James was trying to decide whether or not to let Willie Beasley win, for he was sure he couldn't be beaten. His perfect aim and strong fingers had won him the neighborhood championship for years. He decided to win first and then to let Willie win. He was surprised to find out, however, that letting Willie win was no problem because he really was very good, and James had to play carefully to beat him. It was the first of many games, and in spite of themselves, the boys became fast friends, so James was in no way treated as a prisoner. At first he thought the other prisoners would be angry, but they didn't seem to notice. Sir John was glad that Willie had met someone his own age to entertain him since the trip had turned out to be a long and boring one for the boy. During one of their long days together, Willie asked James to go back to England with him. James instantly flared.

"I'll never be a traitor!" he snapped.

"What difference does it make since you're nothing but a slave in your own country anyway?" asked Willie.

"I am not a slave!" said James angrily. "I was born free."

"Well, you're just a black prisoner now," retorted Willie. "And you have only two choices. You will either be sold as a slave, or you can come to England with me as a friend." He suddenly dropped his belligerent attitude. "Oh, come on, James," he begged. "England abolished slavery. You'll get an education and live in a beautiful home. Father likes you. He thinks you have a fine mind."

James didn't answer. He was tempted, but somehow it didn't seem right. When Sir John sent for him the next day, James stood before him and refused his offer to go to England.

"You must be a fool!" exclaimed Sir John in perplexed anger.

"I am an American prisoner," said James. "I cannot be a traitor to my country."

Willie broke in. "America is not your country, James.

All you are there is a slave."

"I am not a slave," answered James, quietly this time.

"Well, all you are there, then, is a servant," said Willie. "I could understand your loyalty if you were white."

This time James didn't answer.

Sir John sighed. He had spoiled Willie by trying to give him everything he wanted. Now he hated to see him disappointed. In an effort to change James's mind, he said, "You know you'll have to be sold."

James didn't know what to say. He opened his mouth to speak, but changed his mind and said nothing.

"Well?" asked Willie.

"I cannot be a traitor," James answered. Lifting his dark pain-filled eyes and looking directly at Willie, he almost whispered, "I never want to be a slave." He turned and quickly left.

The next day before the prisoner exchange, Willie Beasley approached James.

"You will be transferred to the *Jersey* with the other prisoners," he said. As soon as he started talking, his eyes filled with tears. "It is nothing but a floating death trap. No one gets off alive." He handed James a white envelope. "This is from Father to the captain of the *Jersey.* It will help you. Good-bye, James." He turned and hurried away. Looking down at the white envelope, James realized that Willie was one of the best friends he would ever have. Somehow he knew that they would never meet again.

6

A Prisoner on
the *Jersey*

WHEN James boarded
the *Jersey,* he handed the white envelope to the officer in
charge, who barely glanced at it and waved him on
without comment. He was sent below to the main
prisoner quarters, where his nostrils were immediately
assailed by the loathsome odor of human filth, and all
around the dark hole he could hear the ravings and
groanings of the sick and dying. James knew that he was
probably the only black on board. His mind went back to
Mr. Benezet and his school lessons on how the slaves
were captured and brought to America in the pits of
ships. He now knew just how they must have felt. He
knew why they were so submissive and broken when they
were finally sold. They said that no man sentenced to the
Jersey survived unless he was removed in a short time,
but then, James thought, most prisoners were white. He
thought of his great-grandfather who had survived the
slave ship and of his grandfather who had bought his
freedom. From the number of African slaves in America,
James realized that quite a few of them must have
survived, and in a sudden surge of pride, he realized that

37

he was of the same race. He would make it, too.

When the prisoners were brought on deck the next day, James recognized Daniel Brewton, who looked gravely ill. They were glad to see each other, and because of their past association, they quickly became friends. This relationship was hard on James because Daniel was so sickly that James ended up doing chores and hustling food for both of them. Nevertheless, James was still able to volunteer for extra jobs, and in his usual manner he picked the ones that kept him on deck and out of the stinking hole as much as possible. He loaded supplies, scrubbed the deck, and even volunteered to bring up the corpses of dead prisoners. After the first few times, this task no longer bothered him. Not only did James survive, but he also grew tough.

He never knew if it was the letter Sir John had written that prompted another prisoner to seek him out one morning while he was doing his chores. The man, who was an officer, told James he was being exchanged for a British prisoner and that he was taking a trunk with him that would hold one person. Joy flooded James's heart to think that he might finally escape, but instinct warned him not to tell Daniel. Somehow he felt like a traitor leaving him behind to die. He rudely avoided Daniel the remainder of the day. That night when Daniel sought him out in the dark pit where they usually huddled together and talked about Philadelphia, their mothers and sisters, and old times, James pretended he was sleepy.

"Leave me alone, Daniel!" he snapped.

"What's wrong?" asked Daniel.

"Nothing," James snapped again. "I'm just sick and tired of waiting to get off this boat."

"I don't think I'm ever going to get off," said Daniel. "I don't think I'm ever going to see Philadelphia or my home again." His voice cracked, and James knew that he was crying.

Long after Daniel had fallen asleep, James still lay awake, hating himself for what he knew he had to do. The next morning Daniel did not even want to go up on deck for fresh air, and James had to practically carry him up. His face was gray and his eyelids were red and swollen. His body was covered with sores. His eyes seemed to be constantly pleading with James. That evening James slipped Daniel into the trunk, and the next morning he and the officer carried the trunk down to the waiting boats, which took it and the officer to freedom. As the boat disappeared toward shore, James swallowed hard and fought back the tears, knowing that it was too late to change his mind now and that a golden opportunity had slipped through his fingers.

"I can make it," he whispered to himself. "I know I can make it." He put his hands in his pocket and felt the round hardness of his bag of marbles that he had childishly clung to since leaving home. In sudden anger, he tossed them into the sea. He would never need them again. They belonged to the world of Fred and Larry, and now, Daniel. He felt like a tired old man as he turned back to the *Jersey* and wondered how he could make it through another day.

He did make it through, though. That day and the next day and the next for three more months. Near the end of the war, he was freed in a general prisoner exchange. After the American ship, loaded with returning prisoners, docked in Philadelphia, James walked down the tiny streets of his boyhood home, wondering how the houses and streets could ever have looked so huge. A few people glanced at him curiously, some with recognition, but he barely noticed anyone. He was thinking of his mother and wondering if she knew he was on his way. He knew that even if she did know, she wouldn't be waiting at the door but would be in the kitchen cooking and would try to pretend that his walking through the door after all this time was nothing very exciting. But the smell of biscuits and gravy would soon fill the house, and her singing voice would float from the kitchen. Long before nightfall the whole neighborhood would know that Sarah Forten's boy was home.

James pushed the door open, and the aroma of cooking food filled his nostrils. She knew. When he walked into the kitchen, she didn't even look up until he whirled her around in a bear hug. In spite of herself, she could not help crying when she saw how much James looked like his father. He was now six feet two inches and thin as a rail.

"You're so skinny," she said, shaking her head.

"They don't cook like you do on the *Jersey*," replied James, laughing. "Where is Abigail?"

"Oh, she lives down the street now," said his mother. "There was no way to tell you. She's married."

"Married!" exclaimed James. To him Abigail was just a child. He couldn't imagine her married.

"Daniel Brewton was here and told us how you slipped him off the boat," his mother said. "I'm proud of you." After a moment, when James didn't answer, she went on. "Now that the war is over, you can go and see Mr. Bridges about a job in the sail loft."

"I won't be staying," said James in sudden decision. He hadn't thought about it until now. "I'm going to England."

"England?" said his mother. "Whatever for?"

"There are no slaves in England," he said.

"But you don't have to worry about slavery, James."

"If slavery was abolished in England," he answered bitterly, "maybe it's the best country for blacks to live in. After what I've been through, I can't live in a country where my brothers are slaves."

They were interrupted by Abigail bursting through the door and throwing herself on James. She hadn't grown an inch.

"I hear you're a married woman now." He held her back from him.

"Yes," said Abigail almost shyly. "This is your brother now." Holding her hand out toward the young man who stood by the door, she said, "This is Charles Dunbar." Giggling, she added, "Everybody calls him Dunbar, though."

The two young men shook hands, and James decided that he would probably like this sandy-haired young man with gray eyes and yellowish-brown skin who laughed a lot and constantly teased Abigail.

"Dunbar is a sailor," said Abigail, "and he's been practically everywhere in the world. You should see the things he brings home. Things are much better now." She looked at her mother, busy preparing James a plate.

"Have you ever been to England?" asked James with interest.

"We'll talk about that later," broke in Sarah Forten nervously. "Right now James has to eat. See how skinny he is?"

She piled his plate high with rice and gravy and biscuits and pork chops and okra, just the way James had dreamed of her doing over and over again while he lay in the dark misery of the *Jersey,* counting off the passing days. It had taken 210 days for the dream to come true.

7
England

JAMES was content with his mother's good cooking only as long as it took to regain his strength. And even she had to admit finally nothing was ever going to put much weight on James's lanky frame.

Since Dunbar knew that James was determined to go to England, he managed to get him signed up on the crew of a ship going there. Although James was now a young man of eighteen who had been away from home before, Mrs. Forten was worried. Partly because of her concern and partly because of the adventure of seafaring life, Dunbar decided to accompany James, although he knew Abigail disapproved of his taking such a long journey.

James was filled with anticipation when the boat docked in Liverpool. But his anticipation began to fade as he and Dunbar walked along the wharves searching for lodging and work. Dunbar knew England and carefully steered James away from the more inviting places, pointing out that black men were not welcome. They finally found lodgings and work among the worst taverns and filth of the waterfront.

The work was backbreaking, and the merchants and shop owners were barely courteous to them. James realized that the friendship and companionship he and Willie Beasley had shared on board the *Amphyon* would never have been possible in England. If he had accepted Willie's offer to join his family in England, it would have been as a servant, not a friend, to Willie. When James had left America, he had intended to surprise Willie by just showing up one day. He had imagined the things they would do, the places they would go. Now he realized that Willie Beasley's England could never be his England, and he knew that a common black dockhand appearing at the home of one of Enlgand's most influential families would not be a welcome sight.

Although black men were free in England, it was there that James learned to hate slavery with a passion that knew no bounds. He often walked along the wharves and looked with fascinated horror at the merchandise boldly displayed in the shopwindows for use in forcing slaves into submission. He saw shackles, handcuffs, and whips, but the instrument he despised most of all was a mouth opener that was used to force proud, rebellious slaves to eat and live when they had chosen to starve themselves to death.

James could not understand the need for this type of equipment in a country where all slaves had been freed, but that was before he learned England was the slave-trading center of the world. One of the most profitable businesses of English ships was to transport captured Africans from their native land to America and other parts of the world to be sold as slaves.

He and Dunbar ate in the inn of a West Indian boarding house where they had found lodgings. Evenings always found the inn crowded with sailors and seamen talking about their voyages, often making up stories about where they had been and what they had seen on foreign shores. James and Dunbar usually sat around talking with Eddie, the owner of the inn, whom Dunbar knew quite well from his previous trips to England. James liked being around Eddie because everyone confided in him and brought him news from all over the world. They had just finished eating when Eddie pointed out a short, heavy-set white sailor coming in the door.

"Here comes old Pete," said Eddie. "He says he's my best friend, and before the night is over, he's going to tell me about the slaver *Zong* again."

By the time Eddie had finished speaking, Pete was at the table. Knowing that James and Dunbar hadn't heard the story, Eddie baited Pete right away. "I haven't seen you in so long," he said, "that I thought you had decided to sign aboard a ship again and take a voyage."

"Oh, no," said Pete. "I'm scared to sign up for any boats around here in Liverpool." Turning to James, he said, "You can't tell when you're going to end up on a slaver."

James didn't answer.

"Did Eddie tell you about that time I was on the *Zong?*" asked Pete.

James shook his head.

"You've heard about the *Zong* haven't you?" asked Pete. James shook his head. Pete looked hard at him. "You should have," he said. "It was the crime of crimes against your people."

James had been prepared for the type of fantasy stories that the sailors usually told, but something about Pete's sober tone and studied look made him feel uneasy.

"They all think I'm lying," he said, waving his hand grandly around him. "Even old Eddie, here." He looked

44

accusingly at Eddie, who ignored him. "But believe me, young fellow, it's true." He settled back and began talking.

"The *Zong* came in and loaded up and was supposed to be sailing for Jamaica," said Pete. "I signed up on the crew. Instead of Jamaica, we stopped at a few ports on the way and sold the cargo, and the next thing I knew, we were sailing for the west coast of Africa. We arrived, and there was a regular camp set up where they had all these Africans locked up. They started driving them out of this stockade into the boats. They had them handcuffed or chained, and you could tell some of them had been handled kind of rough. Some were just little kids, and some of the women had little babies. The men must have put up quite a fight because most of them were bruised up. There was one I will never forget. I thought they were going to have to kill him. Even with those chains on, he was still fighting. He acted like he wanted them to kill him. His back was bleeding and his face was all puffy. He had paint or something on his eyes, and that made him look wild anyway. If I ever saw pure hate, it was on his face. They said he was a ruler of some tribe and had been tricked by his own brother and sold."

James was horrified. "Why didn't the Africans attack or something and free the captured ones?" he asked.

"The captives were never from the area," said Pete. "They were kidnapped from all over, from all different tribes and places, and just brought there to be sold to the English. Sometimes they had been sold three or four times by the time the English arrived." Seeing that James was really interested in the story, Pete went on, ever more dramatically.

"The *Zong* wasn't a large ship, but we loaded close to four hundred slaves in the pit. They said that half of them would die anyway. They were right, and before we got to Jamica, some had started catching something that must have been contagious because they were getting sick one by one. The captain told us one day that we were running out of water, and our only hope was to get rid of some of the slaves. Well, I wasn't the only one to speak up, but it didn't do any good, and he insisted that we throw the sick ones overboard."

"How could you?" interrupted James.

"I personally didn't," said Pete. "In fact, just a few of the crew helped. They brought them up ten and fifteen at a time while the rest of us just stood around watching or hiding. Some of the slaves that weren't too sick put up a fight, but they were driven over with whips. If a woman had a sick baby, they'd just throw the baby over, and the mother would more than likely jump over."

By the time he had finished the story, Pete was crying aloud. Eddie poured him a drink.

James felt sick and clammy and suddenly realized that he needed fresh air very badly. He stumbled from the rooming house out into the cold night air. While he stood there, an elderly man wearing a dark cloak and Quaker hat suddenly appeared, it seemed, out of nowhere. He slipped James a pamphlet. James glanced at it, quickly reading the front. It was entitled *A Caution and Warning to Great Britian and Her Colonies* by Anthony Benezet. James was startled to see his old schoolmaster's name and spoke it out loud.

"You know him?" the Quaker asked James.

"He was my schoolmaster," answered James.

"You must be one of the students from his colored school in the colonies," said the Quaker. "Put the pamphlet away quickly and read it only when you are alone," the Quaker warned him. Reaching under his cloak,

he slipped James some more papers. "Don't ask too many questions. The movement has many enemies." He strolled on, leaving James alone with the papers that he was now anxious to read. Hurrying back to his room, James sat up late into the night reading and rereading the pamphlets. For the first time, James became aware that there were men in the world who felt as he did about slavery and that they were doing something about it. He saw why the Quaker was so cautious about being seen with the pamphlets, for the words were dynamite—"murderers," "man stealers," "human cargo"—words that excited and angered. The pamphlets gave the address of a meeting to be held the following evening. When James fell asleep, he dreamed of a proud and strong African prince being captured in a hunter's net and dragged, struggling, to a ship where he was thrown into a dark pit that looked strangely like the one on the *Jersey*. When he was pulled out and the net opened, he had been transformed to a huge, ugly, broken, and humble man and sold as a fieldhand in America. James awakened in a cold sweat and vowed he would be at the meeting.

That night James was welcomed to the anti-slavery meeting, which was attended mostly by white men. When it was found that he was from America, he was asked to comment on the conditions of the blacks in his country. James was embarrassed that he knew almost nothing personally about slavery. He didn't even know any slaves. He cleared his throat.

"I have never been a slave," he said, "and I don't really know any slaves." The men looked at him in obvious disbelief. Feeling a need to explain, James went on. "I have seen," he said earnestly, "that the hate and cruelty that limit slavery to the African race is based only on skin color. This means that *all* men who happen to be born black immediately become an object of hate and scorn. Why should we be judged by our color? Slavery is just the most obvious and the most cruel means of adversity against men whose color falls below the wavering and uncertain shades of white." James was still burning from Pete's story of the *Zong* and the writings he had read the night before. His voice rang out clear and strong. "In America, it is not asked if a man is brave or is he honest or is he just, but is he black? As long as one man remains a victim because of his color, then no black man is truly free." James stopped and suddenly felt very frightened and foolish. He abruptly sat down. He felt as though everyone was staring at him, and they were.

After the meeting, James was invited back and was soon looked upon as a kind of expert on slavery by the small group of men who had vowed to dedicate their lives to freeing their black brothers, not only from bondage, but also from oppression.

Dunbar had been observing James's activities with interest, thinking that he would soon tire of England when he saw that it was not the beautiful, free country for blacks that he had thought it would be. He was sure that James would be making the return trip to America with him on the *Commerce*, and he couldn't believe it when James announced that he was not going back.

"Do you mean that you'd rather stay here in Liverpool than go back to Philadelphia?" asked Dunbar. "I thought that you hated Liverpool."

"I do hate it," said James. "Everytime I load a boat, I wonder if it is a slaver. I find myself looking for evidence to prove that it is."

"Why stay then?" asked Dunbar.

"I don't think I'll stay here," said James. "I'm going to London."

"Why?" asked Dunbar. "I think you're getting too carried away with those meetings you've been going to. There's nothing they can do about slavery."

"They abolished it in England," James answered. "Just through the work of a handful of men."

"They were white men, James. Don't forget."

"I just want to find out how they did it," said James. "Granville Sharp is in London. He is the man most responsible for getting slavery abolished in England, and I'll hear him at the meetings there."

Dunbar shook his head in exasperation. "Well," he said, "what do you want me to tell your mother?"

James laughed. "Just tell her that I'll see her. But you tell Abigail that it's not my fault that you were gone so long." They laughed in mutual understanding.

The next morning James departed for the two-hundred mile ride to London, and Dunbar boarded the *Commerce* and sailed for America. In London, James immediately headed for the waterfront and was soon working again. After his long hours of work, and between meetings, James explored London's streets. What he saw continued to discourage him and made him long for Philadelphia. Thirteen years after the abolition of slavery, English ships boldly carried on their slave trade. Fog covered everything, and even the white people seemed extremely poor compared to those in America. Yet James remained, for he had a cause that made every moment worth while.

The meetings in London were more formal than the ones in Liverpool, and James always felt a little out of place, although everyone was kind. These meetings were often held in the private homes of various members of the movement. James noticed that many of them were quite wealthy, and he did not soon forget the luxury in which they lived. Another thing James noticed was that all of them were educated. Their efforts and success on behalf of abolishing slavery, and now the slave trade, were through the printed word, organized meetings, and the revising of the laws of the land.

One drizzly night as James sat through another anti-slavery lecture, the speaker's words suddenly startled him to sharp attention.

"Those people," said the speaker, "will never be free in this culture. In Africa they were happy. They had not advanced or progressed in the thousands of years since they evolved. Yet now they are captured and trapped inside four walls, forced to wear corsets, forced to wear shoes." James stiffened.

The man's voice rose higher in emotion. "Free them!" he cried. "Would you clip the wings of a bird so that it could not fly? Would you force a deer to eat from the trough? Yet we stand by idly while our countrymen force these blacks to live like men."

The words exploded in James's head: "Like men!"

He stood so suddenly that his chair fell to the floor with a loud crash. In the silence that followed, he walked out of the meeting into the rain in a helpless rage. He wiped away from his cheeks the raindrops that felt like tears. It was always raining here. Suddenly he realized that he hated England. He determined then that he would go back home.

8

Foundation Laid

WHEN James arrived in Philadelphia again, he was mature beyond his twenty years and far less restless. Before going home, he went first to the sail loft to see Mr. Bridges.

"You've grown up, James," said Mr. Bridges. "Now you really do look just like your father."

James couldn't help being flattered. He always felt proud to be compared with his father.

"I've missed you, too," said Mr. Bridges, not realizing until he had said it how true it was. "Are you home to stay this time?" he asked.

"Yes," answered James. "I'm tired of crowded cities, fog, and backbreaking jobs. It's good to breathe Philadelphia's fresh air again."

"You came at the right time," said Mr. Bridges. "I need another apprentice in the loft. Why don't you come work for me?"

James's face lit up in one of his rare smiles. Quickly accepting Mr. Bridges's offer and signing the necessary papers, James started for home filled with a happiness he hadn't known since he was a child when he had met his father at the sail loft in the evenings. When he arrived home, James was shocked to be met at the door by a round-eyed, chubby child who watched him suspiciously as he entered. A moment later, he was greeted by Abigail, Dunbar, and his mother.

"This is your nephew, Thomas," Abigail said, laughing. James picked up the solemn child.

"I didn't realize I had been gone such a long time," he said.

He was soon to discover that many new things had happened in Philadelphia during his absence. On his first Sunday home, James accompanied his mother to church. On the way, they stopped at Larry's house, as their mothers were close friends and always went to church together.

"Why aren't you coming, Larry?" asked James. They, too, had always gone to church together since boyhood.

"Fred and I don't go to church any more," said Larry.

"Oh," said James, thinking maybe they had outgrown it. He himself had very seldom gone to church in England.

"Don't you say anything to James," said Larry's mother as she scurried through the room in the breathless way that James remembered so well. She hugged him close.

"James, it is good to see you home. But don't listen to a word Larry says. You know how he is."

James laughed and winked at Larry. "Yes," he said. "He always has been a bad influence on me."

James lingered behind the women for a moment and questioned Larry.

"What didn't she want you to tell me?" he asked.

"You'll see when you get there," said Larry. "All the black people have to sit in the balcony now."

"That's where you and I always sat," said James.

"I know," said Larry, "but now we have to. All of us."

When James arrived at St. George's, he followed his mother and Larry's mother up the steps to the balcony. Looking around, he searched for Beulah Benford, the fat, grinning black woman they had made fun of when they were children because she always insisted on sitting as close to the front of the church as possible. He finally spotted her dark, unsmiling face in the rear of the balcony. Somehow he felt sorry for her. He also saw Richard Allen, a black preacher who was often called upon to conduct services before James had gone away. Allen was famous for his beautiful voice that held the audience spellbound, but he, too, was ordered to the balcony. James felt a flush of anger as he looked around at all the blacks crowded together in the balcony. They made up over one-third of the membership of St. George's and had helped build it from the ground up. Now they were no longer welcome. James was too furious to sit through services and waited outside.

"Why do you bother coming at all?" he asked his mother as they walked home together afterward. "Why would any black person go there? We're not wanted there any more."

"Your father helped build that church," said Mrs. Forten. "No matter how tired he was after work, he'd go over and work on that building. That church is as much ours as anybody else's."

"We should build another one just for us, instead of giving them our money to treat us like dogs!"

"Stop shouting," said his mother. "We can't do that. It would take years." Becoming more agitated, she asked, "Why should we have to leave our church?"

"If it were ours, we could sit anywhere. I'll never go back."

James fully intended to keep that vow, but Fred and

54

Larry came by a few weeks later and told him that blacks were going to resist the whites at St. George's.

"They say that the whites have said that no more blacks had better come down to the main auditorium again," said Fred.

"Well, they don't have to worry about that," said James bitterly, remembering how submissively the blacks at St. George's had given up their seats. "If they tell them not to go to the front of the balcony, they won't," he added.

"Someone will," said Larry. "They always do."

"I doubt it," said James. Nevertheless, he joined Fred and Larry and the hundreds of blacks that had heard of the smoldering conflict and had come to St. George's. The service was conducted in the usual manner up to the point when the minister called for altar prayer. At that time those in the audience who desired assembled around the altar and knelt to pray. Reverend Richard Allen and his fellow minister, Absalom Jones, went to the front of the balcony, knowing that they had been banished from the main auditorium. They were followed closely by Beulah Benford and several of the older women. A few minutes later, Larry shook James's arm.

"Look!" he whispered.

James saw a young white man grab Absalom Jones by his arm and jerk him. Jones gestured for the man to wait, but the man began pulling him. Someone else grabbed Richard Allen, and in a few moments a small crowd of white people forced the blacks to the back of the balcony.

"Stay here," said one burly, red-haired young man whom James had never seen before and was sure did not even belong to St. George's. He gave Richard Allen a shove that sent him sprawling into James. James jumped from his seat, shoving Richard Allen aside, and before the man could retreat, James sent his fist crashing into the

man's face. The man fell into the arms of his friends. In a moment, Fred and Larry stood on each side of James, and the three of them advanced on the group of white men standing on the steps, but suddenly Richard Allen stood between the two groups.

"Let us not forget this is the Lord's house," he cried.

From the main auditorium, the white minister was calling out the same warning to the congregation, but James was too enraged to heed his plea.

"Get out of the way," he demanded.

"You'll have to fight me first, James," said Richard. He

did not retreat. "What about the women and children?" he asked. "You lead them out of here before there is more trouble."

James looked around him and noticed for the first time the sobbing women and hysterical children.

"The rest of us men will wait until last in case there is any trouble."

"Reverend Allen," called the white minister. "You don't have to leave. This disgraceful incident can be settled quietly." But the blacks filed out of the church in silent anger.

The next day, the blacks assembled in an abandoned blacksmith shop and laid out plans to build a church only

for people of the African race. They all agreed to contribute their time and labor until the church was completed, no matter how long it took. In the meantime, they became members of the Free African Society, which Allen and Jones had organized a few months earlier.

This organization became the center of many activities for the black people once they recognized the freedom they had as a separate organization. As part of the white church, blacks had never been recognized as leaders. They had never spoken out against slavery or oppression, but now a dramatic race-consciousness began to emerge.

James took advantage of this opportunity to distribute the many anti-slavery pamphlets he had brought home from England. He was soon filled with the fire that had possessed him in England as he explained the movement, suggested action to take, and inspired the members. As in England, he was soon recognized as a spokesman for the organization.

Richard Allen and Absalom Jones, too, took on new dimensions as leaders. The two friends were both ex-slaves and both preachers. Their voices rang out in bitterness and anger against slavery, but they differed in their opinions as to the religious affiliation blacks should choose after the St. George incident. The members of the society began to divide into two groups behind them. It was James's work in keeping the anti-slavery issue before them that kept the two religious beliefs from changing the purpose of the society, which had been established to unite black people of all religious beliefs to achieve the common good of all.

Richard Allen was James's greatest inspiration during this period. At one meeting Allen spoke on education. "It is the tool we must fight to possess at all costs," he said. "It is the weapon the white man fights hardest to withhold to keep us in a state of ignorance. Then they criticize us for being ignorant."

Following the meeting, Dunbar, who was illiterate, asked James suddenly, "Will you teach Thomas how to read and write?"

"That's a good idea," James reflected. "Only he's too young now. Maybe in a year or two."

"What about my son?" spoke up Martin, a friend of Dunbar's. "He's seven now."

Before James could answer, several of the other men who were standing around spoke up. Wondering why he hadn't thought about it before, James quickly consented to start a free evening school in his home for black children. In the beginning he felt a bit insecure and found himself copying as well as he could remember the mannerisms of his old teacher, Mr. Benezet. At first he had no trouble keeping an ample amount of work prepared for his students. Soon, however, he found himself searching through bookstores for second-hand textbooks and spending hours teaching himself more advanced skills in English and math so he could stay a suitable distance ahead of this students.

Sometimes he barely had time to eat between his job at the sail loft, his anti-slavery lectures, and the evening classes. Often he stayed up far into the night preparing lessons to teach the next day. The more he studied and learned, the more interested he became in learning. Often he found that he had to go to Mr. Bridges to find out the exact pronunciation of words or the method of working out complicated math problems. Mr. Bridges was a willing teacher, and James's apprenticeship in the sail loft consisted of much more than just learning sailmaking. Soon Mr. Bridges was teaching James almost everything he knew.

9

Lucy

THE YEAR that Dunbar was lost at sea, James met Lucy. She was a fair-skinned girl with long black hair and large, dark eyes. She had smiled at James from across the aisle of the makeshift church that the blacks still used. James was glad that he had come that night. When she stood, he noticed that she was tall for a girl and almost too thin, but still he wished he could meet her. Being far too bashful to approach her himself, James was forced to appeal to Abigail, who had changed in the past few months from a laughing young mother of two husky little boys to a mournful creature whose eyes seemed always to be searching perplexedly for something.

Often when James looked at her, he was filled with anger at Dunbar. Dunbar's wayward ways and adventurous spirit, which made him charming, also made him refuse any work but that of a sailor. After James's own restlessness had been subdued by his travels to England and back, he had worried about the dangerous and adventurous life Dunbar led. Once he had persuaded him to take a job in the sail loft so that he would not have to leave home any more, but Dunbar had grown restless and sullen until he was once again bound for the high seas. Now he was gone forever.

Abigail had stubbornly refused to face the fact that Dunbar was never coming back, even though the remains of his ship had been found months ago. She didn't cry when she had heard, and she didn't tell her sons. The only time James had ever seen his mother and Abigail angry with each other was the day Mrs. Forten had tried to force Abigail to tell the boys their father was dead. Abigail and Mrs. Forten had been sitting on the porch with the children when James came home from the sail loft. When the boys spotted him, they began jumping up and down and calling out, "Hi, Father!"

"Hush, boys," admonished Abigail. "You know that's not your father."

"Where is he then?" demanded little Dunbar, who was noisily impetuous like his mother.

Abigail smiled her faraway smile and said, "Oh, he'll be back any day now. Any day at all."

"Abigail!" exclaimed Mrs. Forten loudly. "You stop that!"

James and Abigail were both startled, for their mother seldom raised her voice.

"Dunbar is dead, Abigail," Mrs. Forten went on. "He ain't never coming back."

"Hush!" whispered Abigail loudly, immediately placing her finger over her lips. Then, grabbing her head in anguish, she said, "Mama, don't say that in front of the kids."

"Well, it's true," said Mrs. Forten again loudly, "and they might as well know it."

"It's not true!" Abigail screamed at the top of her voice. She stood up suddenly and clenched her tiny fists. "Oh, Mama, you're trying to make me cry. I'm going home." Grabbing the two boys by the hand, Abigail practically ran from the porch.

"Abigail! Abigail!" called Mrs. Forten, but Abigail pretended not to hear.

Turning back to James, Mrs. Forten said, "She's got to accept it sometime." Sighing heavily, she went into the house.

James had felt ill at ease around Abigail ever since then. He gave his nephews a monthly allowance, but he never could bring himself to say anything to Abigail about Dunbar.

Looking down at her in church now, James felt the way he had when they were children and he had to ask Abigail for a favor. She would usually do it but always teased him unmercifully first.

"Abigail," said James as he steered her away from the mingling crowds at the reception following the meeting. "Who is that tall light girl who sat across the aisle from us?"

Abigail's placid face lit up mischievously for the first time in months. Pulling her arm playfully away from James and smiling broadly, she asked, "Why?"

"I want to meet her," answered James, knowing Abigail would not let up until she had squeezed every bit of information out of him.

"You do!" she said in mock surprise. "But what about Naomi and Isabel and all the other girls you've been making eyes at all this time?" she asked.

James couldn't help laughing. "You know better than that, Abigail," he said. "Do you know her?"

"She's already married," said Abigail abruptly.

James's laugh died on his lips. "Oh, no," he said. He looked so hurt that Abigail suddenly decided to stop teasing.

"I'm just teasing," she said, relenting. A moment later she was introducing James to Lucy Stevens. James soon forgot the words he spoke then, but he remembered forever that she wore a pink and white dress, spoke in a low, soft voice, and was prettier by far than any other girl he had ever seen.

"I think your school is a wonderful idea," Lucy said. "If you need any help with it, I will galdly do what I can."

James didn't know what to say, but Abigail spoke right up. "Oh, Lucy, that's wonderful," she said. "We need all the help we can get."

Lucy turned out to be much more help than James could have imagined. She could read and write quite well, and soon they had divided the group into two separate classes with Lucy taking the beginners so James could move faster with the more advanced students.

In spite of his great love for Lucy and his work in the school, James was trying hard not to neglect his job in the sail loft, but where once he had put in hours of overtime almost daily, he now rushed home at quitting time like the other employees. One day just about quitting time Mr. Bridges told James that he wished to talk to him about the job. James was a little worried and wondered if Mr. Bridges was angry because he didn't stay late any more, although he seldom took his full lunch period. Or maybe it was about Quincy Carey, the Irishman that Mr. Bridges had hired as an apprentice shortly before he hired James. Quincy hated James and never missed an opportunity to let James know it. Mr. Bridges had always tried to keep his sail loft balanced between white workers and black workers. He took serious pains to keep the balance, and there had never been a color conflict between the men. They knew that Mr. Bridges would not tolerate it. Quincy seemed to get along with the other black workers, so James felt that it was a problem Mr. Bridges would not understand. Besides that, since James was spending more and more time away from the sail loft, Quincy and Mr. Bridges were becoming pretty close friends.

"James," said Mr. Bridges as soon as James approached

him, "I've been wondering how anyone could learn as much about sailmaking as you've learned in the past two years."

"I had a good teacher," answered James, smiling modestly.

Apparently flattered, Mr. Bridges went on. "In two years I can trust you entirely to make the drawings from my measurements. You can cut, sew, and rope a sail faster than I can already, and of all the workers here, you are the only one that can cut accurately for hours without stopping."

James had never heard Mr. Bridges so complimentary and wondered what he had in mind.

"Although you're only twenty-two and the youngest apprentice in my employ," said Mr. Bridges, "because of your skill, energy, and good conduct, I have decided that I want you to take over as foreman of the loft."

"Foreman!" exclaimed James. As long as he could remember, Mr. Bridges had used one of the older men.

"Don't act so shocked, James," said Mr. Bridges, laughing. "The way I look at it, you have as much seniority as any worker here if I count back to the time Thomas Forten first brought you."

Filled with joy, James quickly thanked Mr. Bridges and rushed home to find Lucy. As he approached the house, he could see his mother sitting on the porch. The school had grown so rapidly that there was barely any room left inside for anything else. Although his mother had never complained, James was anxious to move. He thought of the big house he had seen on Shippen Street that had enough room for twice as many students in addition to Lucy and himself—and maybe four or five children of their own someday. As foreman of the loft, there was no need to wait any longer.

10

The Year 1793

JAMES was happy with Lucy, and with his work in the sail loft, in the school, and in the Free African Society's anti-slavery campaign, the years passed swiftly. During the winter of 1793—five years after he became foreman—Robert Bridges became very ill and left James in complete management of the sail loft for a while. Merchants and captains were confronted with dealing with a black person for the first time, and James nervously awaited some negative reaction. When it never came, he finally began to relax. Contrary to his fears of losing business, orders began to increase. Of course, James had to admit this was partly due to the circumstances of that year. The winter was so severe that many ships could not leave the port and used the opportunity to have new sails made or old ones repaired.

In contrast to James's happiness with Lucy and his success at the sail loft in 1793, the conditions of blacks worsened when the invention of the cotton gin killed all hope for a gradual end to slavery. White abolitionists, who had predicted that slavery would die a slow death from lack of profit, had to eat their words as the slave trade tripled.

The increase in the need for slaves to work the expanding cotton fields of the South resulted in the passage of the Fugitive Slave Act in Congress in 1793. This law allowed any white slave owner or his agent, without proof or authority, to seize a black person, accuse him of being a runaway, and return him to a master.

James was wondering how much worse things could get when a yellow fever epidemic swept through Philadelphia, killing thousands. As if providence had intervened on behalf of the oppressed blacks, people of African descent seemed to be immune to the disease.

At this time, the Free African Society, frightened by the Fugitive Slave Act, had chosen James to write an appeal to the authorities of Philadelphia requesting that any black person seized under the new law be given the opportunity to produce papers of freedom or be given a hearing to determine if he was indeed a runaway. James and Lucy printed the name of every person in the society, and beside his name each person entered his signature or scrawled an "X."

The petition was accepted by the Philadelphia government. It displayed the unity of the black people of Philadelphia and inspired the white people a few weeks later to call upon the Free African Society for help with the yellow fever situation. The hospitals were overflowing with victims, and even the doctors and nurses were falling prey to the stampeding epidemic. In desperation, they offered the blacks twice the going wages for nursing care and removal of bodies from the homes of victims. The newspapers carried stories of the medical reasons that blacks could not be infected with the dread disease and printed stories of love and praise for those blacks who volunteered their services.

The leaders of the Free African Society, Reverend Richard Allen and Reverend Absalom Jones, were confused as to the position they should take. Finally, they called for volunteers to aid their white brethren in the name of humanity. Mrs. Forten, Abigail, and many of the women immediately volunteered, but Lucy seemed relieved when James told her he did not want her to help. She was afraid of death, and the sight of any kind of suffering moved her to tears. But as the weeks passed, Mrs. Forten and Abigail showed no signs of becoming ill, and all the women Lucy knew seemed involved in the care of the sick. She began to feel guilty. She finally volunteered to accompany Abigail and Mrs. Forten to the homes of the victims.

A few days later the wives of two black employees in the sail loft died, and in fearful premonition, James immediately sought out the men to ask if their wives had died of yellow fever. They were so filled with grief that they could not answer many questions, but both men assured James that the doctors had told them neither woman had died of yellow fever. For some reason, James just couldn't believe the doctors told the truth.

That evening when James and Lucy arrived at the meeting of the Free African Society, James's sharp eyes noticed immediately that there were fewer people than usual. Obtaining permission from Richard Allen, James asked if anyone in the congregation knew someone who was sick or had died in the past month. Over half the hands were raised.

"It is my opinion, then," said James to the crowd, "that we immediately refrain from exposing ourselves to the disease. We were virtually untouched by the epidemic as long as we kept ourselves from the white race. As soon as we exposed ourselves, we, too, became victims to the fever."

The crowd began to applaud in agreement. Feeling more at ease, James went on. "I know it is said that we are immune, but remember that they do not look on us as human beings with the same strengths and weaknesses as they have. I personally believe that many of us have already died because we trusted their words."

It was just a little speech, but Lucy's eyes were filled with pride when James left the platform. He was glad that he had spoken out, for he did not like to see her as weary and exhausted as she had been when she returned from nursing the sick. As they walked home from the meeting, Lucy suddenly leaned heavily against James's arm. Surprised at what he thought was a sudden display of emotion, James took her hands and was troubled to find them quite warm. During the night, Lucy's temperature climbed so high that in great fear James fled into the night to get his mother, who lived with Abigail and her children since James had married.

Hurriedly dressing, the two women went immediately to James's house, and soon his greatest fear was realized. From her experience with the disease, his mother informed James that Lucy had yellow fever.

James immediately broke down in tears. "I told you," he said to his mother, "I told you that we could catch it. They knew it all the time."

"Don't give up yet, James," said his mother. "Some people make it."

Afraid to hope, James went to work the next day as usual, and the days following. Not knowing what else to do, he worked far into the night, the dread in his heart growing daily. By the sixth day, his own back and chest were aching so badly that he could hardly breathe.

"Why don't you go home?" asked Charles Anthony, one of the black workers from the sail loft.

"I'm afraid to go home because I know Lucy is dead," James answered.

"Don't talk like that, James," cautioned Anthony. "Have a little faith."

James left and walked slowly home to his large house on Shippen Street, the home that he and Lucy had planned to fill with students and babies. His mother met him at the door, and James knew before she spoke that it was all over at last.

"I'm so sorry, James," said his mother. "Just when it seemed she was getting better, she died."

James shook his head and sighed heavily, but he had already spent his grief.

"Well, at least her suffering is over," he said softly.

11

The Promised Land

As if Lucy's death had not made James bitter enough, it was followed shortly by the most slanderous attack on blacks he could have imagined. The same newspapers that had begged the blacks for aid during the epidemic, declaring them immune, now savagely accused them of having committed the vilest of crimes in the homes of the whites. Blacks were accused of everything from extortion to theft. Reverend Absalom Jones and Reverend Richard Allen published a brilliant reply to this attack, but James, weary with grief, would have no part of it.

Later, reading their reply, James saw that they had included in their answer to the white public the fact that the year before only 67 black persons had died while, during the epidemic, 305 had been lost as a result of their compassion toward their white brethren. In the same publication, they pleaded for an end to slavery and oppression for the black man, pointing out that these were robbing his mind, debasing his spirit, and causing insurrections.

In 1794, James's depression and gloom were somewhat

brightened by his meeting Paul Cuffe. He had been walking along the waterfront when he suddenly noticed a boat called *The Mary.* It was a good-looking schooner, and James was surprised to see a black captain and all-black crew. He waited on the landing for the captain to leave the boat, and as soon as he did, James walked up and promptly introduced himself. Normally he would have been more reserved, but his curiosity made him bold.

"My name is James Forten," he said, extending his hand to the captain. "Is this your boat?"

The nut-brown captain quickly returned James's handshake and, smiling in friendliness, answered, "That she is." He did not seem to think James's introduction strange. "I am Captain Paul Cuffe," he said. "We are in Philadelphia to sell whale oil and bone."

"Where are you staying?" asked James.

"We have only just arrived," said Paul.

"Come to my house," said James impulsively. "I have plenty of room."

It was the beginning of a friendship that changed James's life. They first stopped at the house of his mother and Abigail for dinner and then went to the Free African Society meeting. That night at James's home they talked far into the night, and James learned of Paul's great love for Africa.

"My father remembered Africa," said Paul. "He was kidnapped and sold in Massachusetts. My mother is an Indian. The closest Father could come to accepting life in this pagan country was building a house on Chutterhunk Island, where all ten of us were born."

"It seems strange to think of someone who actually remembers Africa," said James.

"Father remembered it well," replied Paul. "He said

that there were trees and fruits in abundance. There was peace, and there the black man had wives, children, homes, and work like all men everywhere else in the world. Not like here in America where they are just . . . just common animals."

"But what about the jungles and the savages?" James asked, and was immediately sorry he had said it. Paul's face lost its dreaminess, and he almost snapped, "They have them here, too!"

"Don't you feel that America is home now, though?" James asked Paul.

"No," said Paul. "This is the land of the white pioneers. They came to this wilderness to tame it and build it up into a dream. We were never included in their plans."

"You're right about that," said James, thinking about the constant struggle of the blacks in America.

"We should leave this oppression," said Paul, "just like they left oppression." Once more his voice became elated. "We should go back to the wilderness of Africa. Build it up. Cultivate it. Teach the natives. Use everything we have learned from them, like they did." He paused a moment. "If they did it, why can't we?"

James didn't answer.

Paul stood up, and looking down at James, who was still sitting, he pushed his shoulders lightly, but his voice was urgent.

"Why don't you want to go?"

"I didn't say that I didn't," said James quickly.

"Well do you?" asked Paul.

"I don't know, Paul," James answered truthfully. After a moment's hesitation he went on.

"I was born here. So was my father. His father bought his own freedom. They weren't intruders here. Their sweat and tears helped build this country. I fought for her freedom during the Revolution." He paused a moment reflectively and then declared, "I guess I feel it's just as much my country as the white man's."

"But the white man will never share America," said Paul. "This is his dream."

"And our nightmare," said James bitterly.

Paul laughed loudly. "You don't know your power, James. At the Free African Society, I notice that you are one of the leaders. I gather you run the sail loft practically alone. You have the gift of teaching. You, James, can lead your people back to the Promised Land."

"I do wish we could all leave this country in a group the way we walked out of St. George's and sail for Africa, but some of us are slaves, and some of us wouldn't want to go."

"You can walk out, James!" Paul said emphatically. "I have talked with the rulers there. They have promised us land. All we have to do is load the boats. The slaves will eventually be freed; besides, there is nothing we can do for them here."

"But what about those that would not want to go?" said James. "They would not leave their homes and go to the other side of the world to a land they think is inhabited by head shrinkers and savages, even though they are our brothers."

Paul was shaking his head sadly while James talked. "Africa is not like that," he said when James had finished speaking. "How long will you listen to the lies of the Americans? They just tell you things like that to make you ashamed. They want you to be grateful for this pitiful existence you have here." Paul sighed deeply. "He's like the devil, the white man," Paul went on. "He will never mean you any good in this country."

"That is so true," said James. "After the yellow fever epidemic, I should know well not to believe his lies."

James told Paul about the epidemic and the lies and the scandal that had followed and of all the blacks who had died, including Lucy. He talked on and on, releasing the pent-up anger and bitterness that he had never admitted until now. When he had finished talking, he had convinced himself that there had to be a separate country for the black race. He consented to serve as the chairman of the American branch of the London African Institute, an organization founded by Granville Sharp to transfer freed slaves to the British colony of Sierra Leone in Africa.

12

The Boss's Job

MR. BRIDGES never regained his vigor after his illness in 1793. He occasionally visited the sail loft, but as his body became frailer, his visits became less and less frequent with each passing year. By 1798, ten years after James had become foreman, no one expected Mr. Bridges to live much longer.

Quincy, in the meantime, had become bolder and bolder. He often wondered out loud to white employees if the next owner would let a common black field hand run his sail loft. James never commented, but he had considered the question himself many times. More than once he had had to work far into the night to meet deadlines on jobs that Quincy had deliberately botched. He could do everything in the sail loft but fire Quincy. Uneasily, James noticed the unrest that Quincy was causing among the white employees with his complaints and remarks.

For some years, now, James had been toying with a gadget he had designed that made the handling of sails easier when attaching them to the masts. Bending and fastening the finished sails to the masts had always been a tedious job, especially on large ships. It was the job his father had been doing when he fell into the river. James knew that at last the instrument was perfected and ready for use, and he had already decided to use his invention to improve his now precarious position in the sailmaking business. He was hoping that it would help him persuade Mr. Bridges to take him on as a full partner.

When James finally got an opportunity to show the device to Mr. Bridges, he was disappointed. Mr. Bridges did not seem impressed. He seemed to have something else on his mind.

"That's very nice, James," he said absently.

"Don't you want to know what I'm going to do with it?" asked James.

"Well, I hope you're going to sell it," said Mr. Bridges, trying to be jovial.

"No," said James. "That would increase our competition. I thought you would be interested in taking me on as a partner. We will be able to make three times the profit we make now."

"That's what I wanted to talk to you about, James," said Mr. Bridges. "I'm through with the sail loft. I'm through with the business. I want to sell out."

"To whom?" asked James in disgust. Although he had known this day was coming, he couldn't believe it would turn out like this.

"There are several sailmaking companies that I think would be glad to buy out my competition," said Mr. Bridges. At James's downcast look, he said, "I'm sorry, James, but I am sure that any of them would be glad to have a master sailmaker like you. Maybe you can even get one of them to use your invention."

James abstractly began roping a sail. He barely answered when, after a few minutes of uneasy conversation, Mr. Bridges bid him good night. James worked late that night as he always did whenever he was troubled. As he left the loft, he practically collided with Mr. Willig.

"Hello, James," said Mr. Willig mildly. "You must have a lot on your mind." He was a humorless man, not much taken to conversation. He was always busy and preoccupied with one of his many interests and businesses in Philadelphia. James apologized and continued walking a few steps in the opposite direction when he suddenly stopped short, stuck with an idea.

"Mr. Willig! Mr. Willig!" called James.

"Oh?" said Mr. Willig. He was puzzled.

"Mr. Bridges is getting ready to sell the sail loft, and I want to buy it," said James. As the two men walked along slowly, James told Mr. Willig about the volume of business, the nature of expenses, future orders, and everything else he could think of pertaining to the sail loft. Mr. Willig listened while James talked.

When James had finished, he said, "You've practically run that loft yourself for years, haven't you, James?" Not waiting for an answer, he continued, "I've never had a chance to tell you how grateful I was for what you did for Thomas. But I'm a businessman, James, and I can never let my personal feelings interfere with my decisions on any business venture. An investment must be a sound one—one that will make a profit."

He didn't say anything more, and the silence grew heavy between them. James could tell that Mr. Willig felt bad. They were now near the sail loft again, and James at that moment said impulsively, "Come into the loft with me for a minute, Mr. Willig. I want to show you something."

Mr. Willig followed him in. James then took out the model he had used to demonstrate his invention to Mr.

Bridges and began demonstrating it to Mr. Willig. Mr. Willig seemed interested, and James carefully explained the device and answered all Mr. Willig's questions in detail.

When he had finished, Mr. Willig said, "You are remarkable, James. Truly remarkable. With that invention you can't help but succeed. The faster and better you service ships, the more your business will increase."

James smiled happily.

Mr. Willig held out his hand to James, and the two men shook hands warmly. "I will make arrangements immediately," promised Mr. Willig. A week later, ownership passed from Mr. Bridges to James. The transaction was so smooth and quiet that most of the employees did not know for months that James was the owner. Only Quincy was informed immediately.

"Do you want me to tell Quincy?" Mr. Bridges asked.

"No," answered James. "Just call him over, and I'll tell him."

"By rights, he ought to be the next foreman in your place," said Mr. Bridges.

James stared at Mr. Bridges silently. Mr. Bridges shrugged his shoulders and called Quincy.

"Quincy," said James slowly while pretending to inspect some rope in his hand. "The last time you made the drawings they were wrong, and the canvas didn't fit the masts."

Quincy's face reddened. He turned to Mr. Bridges.

"What's he talking about?" he demanded. Mr. Bridges looked uncomfortable.

"Furthermore," James went on, still pretending to study the rope, "your complaining about me and your wise-cracks have been causing dissension among the white workers." He then looked Quincy directly in the face and said, "I just can't have that in my sail loft."

"*Your* loft!" exploded Quincy. Again he turned to Mr. Bridges. "What is he talking about?"

"Because of your attitude," said James, "I feel completely justified in making Charles Anthony foreman of the loft in my place rather than you."

"Is he crazy?" Quincy asked Mr. Bridges.

"It's his sail loft now," said Mr. Bridges.

"Well, one thing for sure," said Quincy, "I ain't going to work for no nigger!"

"Then leave now," said James, throwing the rope to the floor. Quincy turned and fled the loft. James laughed aloud, and Mr. Bridges could not help but smile.

"Your father would be proud of you, James," he said. "How many years ago was it that you first came here with him?"

"Twenty-three years ago," said James reflectively. "I was just nine years old."

"You worked hard that day," said Mr. Bridges. "And you've never changed in that way."

"You paid me a shilling," said James with a laugh, "and told me that someday I would have your job."

"So I did," said Mr. Bridges. "So I did." He stood up to go. "Now it's all yours, James."

James watched him as he slowly walked out the door. He was a very old man.

13

Underground and Overboard

In 1800, two years after purchasing the business from Mr. Bridges, thirty-four-year-old James Forten owned the largest and most profitable sail loft in Philadelphia.

In the meantime, the Free African Society had produced two powerful black churches. James followed Absalom Jones, who had organized St. Thomas, and moved his school from his home to the new church. He remained active in the Free African Society, which now met in Richard Allen's church, Bethel. Although James had not changed at all, as his wealth accumulated he found that he did not fit in as before. The whites of Philadelphia felt he was different from the other blacks but still did not welcome him to their homes, and the blacks felt that he was far too advanced to be included as part of their struggle. He was treated with respect by all, yet he was very lonesome.

Seven years after Lucy's death, he still lived alone in his house on Shippen Street and seldom had visitors, so he was shocked one night when he was awakened by the insistent knocking of someone at his back door. When he got to the door, he was even more surprised to see his old friend Larry. They rarely saw each other now, and when James did approach Larry or try to talk to him, Larry acted so secretive and noncommittal that James had finally given up trying.

"Larry Williams?" asked James, not quite believing his eyes.

"Let me in quick!" said Larry.

James stood aside. "What's wrong?" he asked. "What has happened?"

"Lee Tate is outside with Fred. We need your help."

"You know you can count on me," said James immediately. His answer seemed to take Larry by surprise. He and James exchanged looks that wiped away the distance that had grown between them over the past years.

Larry went to the door and whistled loudly. A moment later, Fred and another young man ran into the house. The other man was a dark brown, slender youth with black, tightly curled hair.

"This is Lee," said Fred. "When he came home from work this evening, before he could get in the house, he saw these two white men coming at him from the shed in the backyard."

"I knew they were slave hunters when I saw them," cut in Lee. "I ran in the house and locked the door. I got my gun and started firing at them. Then, lucky for me, Larry and Fred came by." His voice started to tremble. "They weren't going to take me alive," he said harshly. "I'll never go back."

"Are you a slave?" asked James.

"I'm freed, but I don't have no papers," Lee said. "One day Mr. Flanders just came and told me I could go. I been trying to work so I could get my wife and boy. Mr.

Flanders got a mean son. My wife is a fine-looking woman."

"He'll have to stay here tonight, James," said Larry. "Tomorrow we'll get him out of Philadelphia."

"Where to?" asked James.

"Canada," Fred answered.

James was thinking about Lee's wife and Mr. Flanders' mean son.

"What about your family, Lee?" he aksed.

Lee shrugged.

"I'll get them for you," said James. He couldn't stand the thought of Lee's never seeing them again. Turning to Larry, he said, "Larry, come by the sail loft tomorrow. I will have everything ready."

The next day James asked Mr. Willig for the name of a lawyer, and Mr. Willig referred him to Sidney Brown, a young and upcoming lawyer whom James like immediately. Before the morning was over, James had arranged with Sidney to purchase Lee's wife and son from their owner in Virginia. As soon as the purchase was complete, James set them free.

For the first time in years, he felt that he was once more involved in the struggle for freedom. Remembering the zeal of the abolitionists in England, James was ashamed of his lack of effort the past several years. He still corresponded with Paul Cuffe, but Paul's plan to set up a colony for blacks in Africa was still only a dream. As chairman of the American branch of the London African Institute, there was little that James could do but wait.

And the Free African Society was facing many defeats. When Representative Robert Wahl had presented their mild petition against the Fugitive Slave Act, the slave trade, and slavery to Congress, it caused a great stir among the country's lawmakers. Congress, however, felt that the mild petition created disquiet and jealousy and did not bring it up for vote.

But the Lee Tate incident triggered James's thinking about the more immediate solutions to slavery. He insisted that Larry include him as an agent of the Underground Railroad. From that time on, his house always seemed to be filled with slaves escaping from the south to Canada or New York or sometimes even staying in Philadelphia. At night when James heard a knock on the door, he would open it and light the fire. Often the fugitives were alone without Fred, Larry, or one of the other agents and would not even explain how they had been directed to James's house or how they had escaped. He was appalled at the condition in which many of them arrived. They sometimes had no shoes or adequate clothes or were ill and distrustful. Some of them carried weapons. They usually stayed until the following night, when they passed on to the next stop. Being quite well off, James became the contact person for two sea captains who made regular stops in Philadelphia, and each trip brought several escaping slaves. James always paid the required fare and sent them to his home.

One day, a stocky, very fair black man arrived at the sail loft. Walking straight up to James and extending his hand, he said, "My name is Lonnie Anderson."

"Glad to meet you," said James, returning the man's handshake and wondering what he wanted. "May I help you?" he asked.

"Oh, not in particular," the man answered nervously. "I was just supposed to tell you about a box that is coming."

"Oh," said James. It was not unusual for him to be alerted when certain packages arrived, for they were sometimes important. This man, however, made no attempt to leave.

"I'm very busy," James told him.

"Oh, I don't mind," said Lonnie. "I won't be in the way. Go right ahead."

James sighed in exasperation. He didn't want to be rude. He turned sharply and went about his work. Although the man did nothing in particular, his presence was irritating to James.

Later, Lonnie said, "I understand you're the best man in Philadelphia to know these days."

"What are you talking about?" James demanded. He kept his work with the Underground Railroad strictly secret.

"Oh, nothing," replied the man quickly. "This box . . ."

"What about the box?" James interrupted shortly, and was immediately sorry, for Lonnie looked hurt and even more nervous.

"I think I'll wait outside," he said.

"You don't have to," said James half-heartedly, but the man left and James soon forgot him and his box. Hours later when all the workers had gone home and James was preparing to leave, he heard a commotion outside. He ran to the door to see two men struggling with an apparently very heavy box. From somewhere, Lonnie was giving orders.

"Take it easy," he cautioned the two men. "Don't drop it."

"Mr. Forten," asked one of the men, "can't we just leave it down here to be unloaded?" He was sweating profusely.

Before James could answer him, Lonnie said quickly, "No!" Then turning to James he said, "Mr. Forten, remember I told you that this was valuable material?"

"Bring it up," said James. The men heaved again and

finally deposited the box in the middle of the floor.

As soon as the door closed behind them, Lonnie started opening the box.

"Lock the door," he cried. Not understanding, James obediently locked the door.

"What is in there?" he asked.

"Not what," said Lonnie, "but who. It should be Jim Sharpe."

"A man!" exclaimed James in disbelief. He started at once to help Lonnie unseal the crate.

The crate had been exceptionally well sealed, and James realized that not a sound had come from the box. With trembling hands the two men opened it.

"Oh, God!" exclaimed James, covering his face. The man in the box was dead. He had apparently suffocated. The few air holes had been covered when the shippers who received the box were informed that it contained valuable merchandise. The expression on the dead man's face was one of such pain and agony that James knew his suffering must have been great.

He and Lonnie both ran out into the fresh air blowing in from the Delaware. When James could speak again, he asked, "Who was he?"

Lonnie's voice was flat and hard. He didn't sound like the same man who had half apologetically annoyed James earlier that day. "Just an escaping slave who didn't make it," he said. "Don't worry about the body," he added quickly. "Me and my sons will move it."

James nodded. As Lonnie walked away, leaving him standing alone in the darkness, he suddenly became nervous and frightened. He didn't want to be alone.

"Wait, Mr. Anderson," James called. Lonnie waited.

"I'll come with you."

"It's quite a walk from here," Lonnie warned, and

James sensed that he did not want him to come along, but he walked on with him silently, remembering how Lonnie had insisted on staying at the sail loft in spite of his efforts to get rid of him. The circumstances were so ironic that, in spite of his gloom, James chuckled aloud.

"What's wrong," snapped Lonnie.

"Today you tried to be friendly with me and I didn't want to be bothered," said James. "I tried everything to induce you to leave me alone, but you insisted on staying. Now the tables are turned. I'm trying everything to be friendly with you, and now you don't want to be bothered."

"Oh no," protested Lonnie. "It's not that. It's just that we're poor folk. The house is really kind of run down and not fit for a man of your position." James was really taken aback. It continued to puzzle him that most blacks no longer identified with him. They always treated him as if he were white. He made no further attempt at conversation. When they arrived at Lonnie's house, James was amazed that so many people could live in such a small place. Lonnie had the best-looking family James had ever seen. His wife was plump and had long wavy hair that she wore parted in the middle and pulled up in a large knot. She was reddish-brown and had even white teeth. Lonnie's children were various shades between his own olive color and his wife's red-brown and ranged in age from about five or six to the oldest girl, Charlotte, who looked to be in her early twenties.

"This is James Forten," said Lonnie as he followed his wife into the kitchen.

His wife beamed and continued setting the table. "You don't look like you just got out of a box," she said.

"Oh, Mother," said Charlotte in embarrassment. "He's Mr. Forten, the one the box was delivered to."

"Where is the man . . . " Mrs. Anderson started.

"Dead," her husband interrupted. "Someone sealed the air holes."

"Oh, no," said Charlotte and her mother in unison.

"The boys will have to come and help me get the body out of Mr. Forten's shop," said Lonnie.

"It must have been terrible," said Mrs. Anderson. She shook her head and then began filling the plates. James noticed that, unlike her daughter and husband, she was completely at ease. "You sit down on this side of the table, Mr. Forten," she said. "Lonnie can sit on the other side."

"Ma," said Lonnie uneasily, "we got to go."

His wife put her hands on her hips. "Why can't you let Mr. Forten eat before you go? He's upset. Everybody else that comes to this house eats, so what are you rushing off for tonight?"

"Ma," put in Charlotte, "Mr. Forten is not like everybody else. He's a very important man."

"I'll be very glad to stay," James spoke up. "I'm not in the least bit anxious to go back to the sail loft."

"See." Mrs. Anderson smiled in triumph. "Charlotte here and her pa, they're so biggity, they think everybody is biggity."

Lonnie laughed in response, but Charlotte's face shone in embarrassment. Soon the table was filled with Lonnie's other children, and the meal was one of the most pleasant James had had for a long time. You could not long be a stranger in Lonnie's house, for it was a house of laughter and teasing. Before they could leave to return to the sail loft, Mrs. Anderson made James promise to come back.

"Oh, I will definitely come back to see you, whether your husband or daughter want me to or not," said James with a laugh.

"Tell me something more definite than that," Mrs. Anderson insisted. "I want to know exactly when so I can really show you how good Ma Anderson can cook. That stuff I threw together tonight makes me ashamed."

So James promised to come back the following Sunday, and he did. Soon he was spending almost every Sunday at the noisy Anderson household, and everyone assumed that it had to be the fair beauty of Charlotte, with her light brown curls and quick laugh, that was drawing him like a magnet. And it was hard for James and Charlotte to remember the day they ceased being friends and became sweethearts. It was as natural as the fact that spring follows winter, bringing life and beauty with it once again. At last the coldness that had formed around James's heart when he lost Lucy began to melt, and feelings that he had thought long dead came bursting forth in new life.

James had the largest and finest house in all Philadelphia built on Lombard Street for Charlotte's wedding gift.

14

A Man of Power

JAMES was master of a unique home in Philadelphia. He was more active than ever in the Underground Railroad, and the appearance of strangers in his home, although often suspected, was never questioned. The Fortens had many friends and friends of friends who frequently resided in their large mansion. As many as twenty-two people were listed in the city directory under his address. Whenever runaway slaves were being housed, they were often mistaken for house guests.

Charlotte had inherited her mother's natural friendliness and ease, which made her a gracious hostess. Even though she boasted one of the most elegant homes in the state, the warm atmosphere that had dominated her mother's humble cabin also pervaded the luxurious Forten household.

James's friend, Paul Cuffe, was doing equally well as the owner of a fleet of ships. He had been around the world several times, yet nothing had ever dimmed his dream of establishing a colony in Africa. The two friends did not see each other often, but James always welcomed the times when Paul was in Philadelphia and they could get together again.

In so many ways they were very much alike. They were both successful businessmen, and Paul now shared James's enthusiasm for education. He had built the schoolhouse and paid the teacher's salary for the first public school in Westport, Massachusetts, where he and his family lived. But the two friends had begun to differ in their ideas as to what direction was the best for the black man.

In 1804, ten years after their first meeting, James and Paul continued to be pulled farther apart in their convictions. Paul was more dedicated than ever to establishing an African colony for black Americans, and his efforts were getting increased support from the British, who were eager for their colony, Sierra Leone, to succeed. James, on the other hand, was so involved in the immediate abolition of slavery through his work in the Underground Railroad that he saw the return to Africa as only a remote possibility in the distant future. For him, the United States was the battleground and freedom was the prize. He was determined to stay and fight until that prize was won.

One evening James and Richard Allen were sitting on the back porch of James's home, removed from the gay laughter and noise that forever echoed from the house. James had just introduced Allen to one of his guests, a young African whose education was being sponsored by the London African Institute. He was not prepared for the anger that Allen showed after the boy went back in the house. In the twilight, the shadows falling on his stocky body made him look as if he were swelling in anger.

"James," he asked through tight lips, "why establish a colony in Africa when the slave trade is still going so strong? As fast as we would leave the country, boats would be bringing in more blacks to be slaves. In fact, as soon as they leave the jurisdiction of this country, they stand the risk of being captured on the high seas and sold into slavery."

"Yes," agreed James, "but look at the oppression in this country for even the free blacks, especially in the South. Since Gabriel Prosser's attempted revolt, the treatment of blacks has become even more harsh. They'll make blacks pay for that revolt for the next twenty years."

"It just proves that violence is not the answer," said Allen. "Seven hundred thousand blacks all united could never overthrow the five million whites in this country."

"I just can't understand why a slave was the one to betray him," said James.

"He loved his master," replied the other quietly. "Does that seem strange to you?"

"Well, they'll never love us. Oppression won't stop when slavery is ended."

"Africa is still not the answer."

"At least it is not a crime to be black in Africa."

"But what about the slaves, James? The free black man is their only hope."

"Oh, I know that colonization can't take the place of abolition," said James quickly. "But there should be a country where slaves can go when they are free—a country where they will not just be free without jobs or land or homes, but a commercial country where African products can be sold and goods from all over the world exchanged."

"Well," Richard Allen admitted, "it sounds good, but it just couldn't be that easy."

"What did the English do?" James asked. Not waiting for an answer, he went on. "They set up trading posts.

They transported people here. They gave settlers land and began exchanging products. Africa is the richest land in the world. Trading will not be a problem."

"It took a hundred and fifty years to throw off England's rule, too, James. Sierra Leone still belongs to the British, not to the blacks who were sent there. Besides, I know that most blacks will not want to leave America."

"The slaves would probably welcome it."

"Let's stop arguing about it," Richard said abruptly, suddenly restored to his usual understanding self.

The two friends bid each other good night unaware of the terror that would soon grip them. As Richard Allen walked from James's home, he was confronted by two men who accused him of being a runaway slave. Newly arrived from the South, they obviously did not realize that they had chained the most loved black man in Philadelphia. They placed him in jail overnight, but word spread like wildfire that Richard Allen was being held. Crowds of blacks soon stood outside the courthouse and refused to leave.

As soon as James heard, he called on Sidney and offered to buy Allen's freedom immediately.

"It's not a matter of money at this point, I'm afraid," Sidney responded. "It's a matter of principle. They have got to prove that they were within their rights to claim him under the Fugitive Slave Act. Opinion is divided all over the city, and the whole situation is dangerous. Fortunately, in Philadelphia there must be a hearing to determine whether or not he is a slave." Sidney did not know that James had written the petition that made the hearings possible in Philadelphia.

James sighed. There was nothing to do but see what would be determined at the hearing. He stopped by

Abigail's house to warn her to keep Dunbar and Thomas at home because of the angry mood in the city.

"What are you going to do, Uncle James?" Dunbar asked him. "You can't let them take Richard Allen down south and sell him."

"There will be a hearing tomorrow," said James. "If he's not freed then, I don't know what I can do."

"You can have them killed," Thomas shouted. "You have enough money. They are nothing but . . . "

Abigail's hand shot out, striking Thomas in his mouth.

"Don't you ever say anything like that," she warned.

Thomas nodded, but his eyes were still angry. James knew how he felt. On the way home he wondered what he would do if Allen was not freed in the hearing. In his anger, he knew that he was capable of anything to prevent Allen from being taken away. At the same time, he knew how Richard Allen reacted to voilence. Allen would rather go with the white men.

Absalom Jones was waiting for James when he arrived home. "It is time that we put the Pennsylvania Anti-Slavery Society to the test," he told James. "Let us go to see Dr. Benjamin Rush."

The Pennsylvania Anti-Slavery Society was the white abolitionist society in Philadelphia. It was composed of well-to-do men who opposed slavery on a moral basis. The organization relied on persuasion rather than power to end slavery. They used such tactics as refusing to buy slave products, paying for slaves' freedom, and working for legislative reform.

Dr. Rush was glad for the opportunity to act against the Fugitive Slave Act. "The law is unjust," he said, "and this is the way to prove that it won't be tolerated in Philadelphia. Not only will Richard Allen be free, but those men must be punished as a warning that we won't take kindly to such invasion in the future."

Richard Allen was promptly freed at the hearing, and the kidnappers were sentenced to six months in jail. James was convinced that the reason the law had been on their side was because the whites had intervened on their behalf. This incident, more than anything else, impressed on him the need of white support in the black man's cause. As Richard Allen had pointed out, blacks were outnumbered, but in the early 1800's the black man had few white friends willing to close the gap between the white and black races in the new nation.

15

The Registration

O<small>N</small> A dreary, incredibly cold New Year's Day in 1811, James Forten stood on a wharf on the Philadelphia waterfront. The freezing wind cut through his expensive overcoat, chilling him to the bone, while he watched a small brave group of black pioneers board Paul Cuffe's boat, the *Traveller*. They were sailing in the desperate hope of surveying the continent they believed to be their home. James felt an inexplicable sadness at their departure. Paul shook his hand tightly, and as if he sensed James's misgivings, he said in relief, "At last. At last we've done it. It doesn't matter how long it takes now, we have founded us a country. It makes no difference that it may be years before it is accepted. We've been redeemed."

James nodded his head in agreement but could not force himself to smile. If he had only been wiser seventeen years before when he had first met Cuffe, maybe he could have persuaded him to wake up from his dream. He knew it was too late now to even try. He watched the *Traveller* until it was just a speck in the distance and then turned toward home, a happy place for him that the troubles of the outside world could never penetrate. The past ten years had brought many changes in his life, and he seldom thought of the deserted house that still stood on Shippen Street and the lonely years he had spent there after Lucy's death. Charlotte had presented him with a lovely baby girl the year after their marriage, and James forced everyone he knew to agree that she was the most beautiful and wonderful human being ever born.

As Sarah Forten had held the tiny baby in her arms, she smiled happily as she told James, "I've waited a long time to see your child, James. I was afraid that you had given up living after Lucy died. Now that I see you're all right, I can rest in peace."

"Don't talk like that," James had said uncomfortably, but Sarah Forten's words were uncannily true. Before Margaretta was two, her grandmother died in her sleep. James called the daughter born a few months later Sarah, after his mother. Following on Sarah's heels, a year later, Harriet, the true beauty of the family, was born. Charlotte insisted on calling the Fortens' first son James, Jr., and James named the next boy Robert Bridges after the man who had been so like a father to him. The next child was a girl called Mary Isabella, followed by another boy, Thomas. Now in the winter of 1811, there was one more child on the way.

As James walked home through the snow that cold New Year's Day, however, his own prosperity was forgotten as he noticed the idle, poorly dressed blacks walking around with shovels, hoping to be employed to clear the walk by one of the shopowners. Their number seemed to be increasing every day. Philadelphia was the largest city in the state of Pennsylvania, where slavery had been abolished in 1780. Because of the Free African Society,

Philadelphia had a reputation for having the best-educated and wealthiest black population in the nation and was becoming known as a haven for recently freed slaves.

James was disturbed at the reaction their presence was causing in Philadelphia. The whites wished to limit the number of ex-slaves in the city, and the more prosperous blacks resented their presence because they knew that any action whites took against the poor blacks would also affect them. James was especially concerned that successful blacks not forget that the oppression all blacks experienced was because of the color of their skin.

James's fears were soon realized when, a year later, the whites of Philadelphia decided to take action against the rising number of blacks in the city. They submitted a bill in the Pennsylvania State Legislature that would require all blacks passing through or living in the state to register.

At first the blacks were not aware of the far-reaching effects of the Registration Bill because of their involvement in the War of 1812 against the British. It was an unpopular war, and very few white men would volunteer. Only the blacks volunteered in numbers. In the beginning they were not wanted, but as the months dragged on, they were soon welcomed. Finally, blacks comprised over 30 percent of the fighting forces and earned unheard-of praise for their victories. The whites of Philadelphia were so unconcerned about the war that when word reached Philadelphia that the British planned to invade the city, it created a state of near panic. James Forten stepped to the forefront of the public eye when he organized 2,500 black men of the city to defend it against the attack that never came.

By the time the emergency was over, the Registration Bill had passed the lower house of the legislature and was before the Senate. James realized that the danger from this

bill was worse than a British invasion. He met immediately with Richard Allen and Absalom Jones of the Free
African Society. Several of James's other friends were also
included in the meeting. Among them were Larry
Williams and Fred Saunders of the Underground Railroad,
Francis Devanney, a brilliant young apprentice from the
sail loft, and John Gloucester, an ex-slave who was a
house guest at the Fortens. James had more respect for
these men than for any he had ever met. Each of them
was active in the abolition movement, and all had helped
him to organize the militia to protect Philadelphia.

James explained to them that the Registration Bill
would put into effect the same kind of controls used on
free blacks in the South. A man's color would indicate
that he was a slave unless he could prove otherwise. The
burden of proof for his liberty would be in his
registration papers. The papers would be numbered,
registered, and issued by the courts and would give the
name, a physical description, and the way in which
freedom had been attained. Without his papers, any black
man would be considered a runaway slave.

"I don't know whether you realize it," James told the
group, "but this registration bill could ruin me. Not only
would I be forced to register visitors, family members,
and servants, but also land and property."

"It's absurd," said Richard Allen. "Nowhere in the
legends of tyranny has there been such a situation as this,
that a man must account for even existing."

"'The law will be a state law,'" James read from the
papers before him, "'requiring all Negroes to register with
the state. Any Negro coming into Pennsylvania must be
registered within twenty-four hours or face fine, imprison-
ment, and possible sale.'"

"Sale!" exclaimed several of the men in unison.

James read on grimly. "'Authority is to be given to sell for a term of years the services of those Negroes convicted of crimes, and a special tax is to be levied on the free Negroes for the support of their poor.'"

"Why are we not considered men?" said Richard Allen. "The God who made the white man and the black man has left no record declaring us a separate species. We are sustained by the same power, supported by the same food, hurt by the same wounds, but we cannot enjoy the same liberty and be protected by the same laws."

"Yet the Declaration of Independence says all men are created equal," put in Absalom Jones.

"The same man who wrote that," spoke up Francis Devanney, "also said that the black man must be removed beyond all reach in order that his blood might not stain that of his master."

"That disdain of our color is apparent from this section," said James, still reading aloud. "'Any black, whether vagrant or man of character, who cannot produce a certificate of registration is to be arraigned before a justice who is thereupon to commit him to prison.'"

"For being black, I guess," put in Larry.

James read on, "'The jailer is to advertise a freeman and at the expiration of six months, if no owner appears for this degraded black, he is to be sold. If not sold, then he is to be confined to seven years of hard labor.'"

"How in the name of God can an owner appear for a man that is free?" asked Larry.

"That clause is for sport," said Fred Saunders with a laugh. "I can just hear one of those low-down constables if he happens to spot one of us from a distance yelling, 'Hey, stop that Negro.' Then all the youngsters will join in the chase, and from a hundred voices the whole city street will soon be calling, 'Ho, Negro. Where is your certificate?' "

The other men joined in Fred's joke, but their laughter was grim.

"We must warn the people of the danger we are in," said Absalom Jones. "They must understand this means that even if their brother or a friend comes to visit from another state in the Union, they must register him."

"That's crazy," cried Fred. "You'd be a traitor to our race if you did something like that. Slave catchers could find out everything about a man from the registration list. They could follow him home when he left the state and show up at his door at any time. His life would be in constant danger."

"What about children?" asked John Gloucester.

"There are no exceptions," said James. "Within twenty-four hours of birth, they would have to be registered."

"How are we going to fight it?" asked Absalom Jones.

"I think that the best thing to do now is to make it public and try to make people aware of what is happening. If public opinion against the bill is high enough, the Senate will not pass it."

James started working on the publication that night. He financed it himself and released it under the title, *Letters by a Man of Color.*

It was a timely and effective weapon in 1813. The idea of James Forten—the man who had raised a militia of 2,500 men to protect the city of Philadelphia—being subjected to registration was a little too much for even the warmest supporters of the bill. It was quietly defeated.

16

A Stolen Dream

PAUL CUFFE had discovered in his initial voyage to Sierra Leone that the colony begun by the British abolitionists was not successful. From there he had made a trip to England to seek additional support for the colonists, returning to Sierra Leone before sailing for America. He arrived in the United States at the beginning of the war with England. The financial strain had been severe, and he had been treated suspiciously by the governments of both countries. He was not permitted to make another trip to Africa until the war was over in 1815. In spite of his rigorous campaigning on behalf of the colony, only thirty-eight passengers accompanied him to Sierra Leone.

At first James was moved with compassion by Cuffe's failure until he became aware of the chain of events the small group of emigrants set in motion. In December of 1816, a group of prominent white men met in Washington, D.C., to discuss the problem of the free black people in the United States. In the group, composed of men well known in public life, were Thomas Jefferson and Francis Scott Key, both of whom made no secret of their feeling that the black man was inferior. Thomas Jefferson declared that time and experience had taught him that although blacks were more gifted in music and equal in morals, they lacked artistic, oratorical, and poetic talents as a result of their nature and not their condition of oppression. Francis Scott Key, who had paid homage to the land of the free in his poem, "The Star Spangled Banner," suggested that any black person revolting or any white person helping a slave escape should be put to immediate death.

Other members of the group were rich Southern slave owners. They felt the free blacks made the slaves restless and eager to escape and revolt. Also present were a number of true humanitarians. One of these men was Robert Rush, the son of Dr. Benjamin Rush who had often rallied to the aid of blacks in Philadelphia. Another was the Reverend Robert Finley, a close friend of Paul Cuffe. The latter had convinced Finley that returning to the land of his ancestors would be the fulfillment of life for the black man.

This group organized the American Colonization Society, which received immediate support from the federal government. Paul Cuffe had been given so much assistance from the London African Institute and the governor of Sierra Leone that the United States government felt it necessary to intervene at this point rather than contribute to the success of a colony belonging to an enemy nation. The government appropriated $100,000 to establish an American colony in Africa.

James was dismayed when he heard of the organization. He wondered how men who claimed to feel so many different ways about the black man could all come to the same conclusion—to keep the slaves and deport the free blacks.

Black leaders were angry and apprehensive. Richard Allen sought James out at once. "Absalom and I have written some resolutions that we are presenting to the American Colonization Society on behalf of the blacks of Philadelphia," he said.

This was the first time in their long friendship that Richard Allen and Absalom Jones had made definite plans without including James.

"I'm sorry," apologized Allen, noticing James's hurt look. "We will fight colonization to the bitter end, even if it means opposing your friend, Paul Cuffe, publicly. We need you now, James. Many people will follow you. Unless you make your position clear, you'll hurt us."

"What are the resolutions?" asked James.

"For one thing," Richard responded, "we are replying to the colonizationists' charge that free blacks are a dangerous and useless part of the community. You, more than anyone, know that in spite of all the disadvantages we live under, in the hour of danger we always forget the wrongs of our country and rally to her protection."

James nodded his head in agreement.

"The second thing is that we free blacks will never separate ourselves voluntarily from the slave population of this country. They are our brothers, and we would rather be deprived with them than gain a few small advantages by deserting them without hope in bondage."

James was silent.

"Finally," Richard said, "it was agreed that without arts, sciences, and a proper knowledge of government, which we have been consistently denied, the return to the wilds of Africa is a return to perpetual bondage."

"What should I do?" asked James.

"Speak at the meeting we've called, James."

When James arrived at Bethel Church, a crowd of over

three thousand people was there. All of them unanimous-
ly agreed to refuse any attempts to exile them from their
native country. James chaired the meeting.

James wrote to Cuffe after the meeting, explaining why he
felt that at this time he had to oppose colonization in Africa.
He tried to explain that the white man in America was
using Cuffe's beautiful dream as a tool to deport free
blacks and that a project like his depended on the
people's freedom of choice. But he never received a reply.
Several months later, James received a letter from Paul
Cuffe's family saying that he was gravely ill. The next
communication that he received from them told him that
Paul had died on September 9, 1817.

Though greatly saddened by Paul Cuffe's death, James
became more determined than ever to oppose colonization.
In spite of his public position, however, men from the
American Colonization Society visited him in his sail loft
to offer him the highest post available in the new African
colony.

"My name is Mr. Thomas, and I'm from the Colonization Society," the spokesman introduced himself to James.
James disliked him immediately. He was a short, plump
man who smiled constantly and nervously tapped his face
with a large white handkerchief as he talked.

"You have been selected to be the leader of this
heaven-born colony established in Africa," he said to
James, "and I know you will be grateful to take part in
making Paul Cuffe's dream a living reality."

"The plans you have and the plans Paul had for the
establishment of the colony are worlds apart," said James.

"I don't understand," replied Mr. Thomas. "Paul's plan
is certainly the one that we have adopted."

Looking at their bewildered faces, James softened
momentarily. "I know you mean well," he said.

"Your position would be equivalent to that of President of the United States," continued Mr. Thomas. "Because of your close affiliation with Paul Cuffe, we were sure you would accept."

"No, thank you," James responded politely.

"I don't understand," said Mr. Thomas, dabbing his face repeatedly. "Slavery is so oppressive, so degrading . . ."

"But," said James, "your colony is not for slaves. It is for free black people."

"But that's where we will send the slaves when they are freed," Mr. Thomas informed him. "What is the use of freeing them now if they have no place to go?"

"I don't believe you'll ever free them," said James. This timid, nervous, and apparently sincere man was making him angrier than he would have believed possible.

"I resent that," cried Mr. Thomas, dabbing his face furiously. "Our motives are trustworthy and even constitute a gesture of apology for the wrong that has been done to your people. We realize that a great wrong has been done, and we are trying to take corrective measures, although I personally feel that we shouldn't take all the blame for your condition. You yourself know that there is a difference between the races, that the poor slaves could never . . "

"Become useful members of this society like the wealthiest sailmaker in Philadelphia," James finished for him dryly.

"Oh, no. No. That's not what I was going to say," Mr. Thomas said, standing suddenly. "I seem to have done everything wrong. I didn't mean to insult you. I was just trying to be helpful." He held his hand out to James. James shook it briefly.

"Mr. Forten," said Mr. Thomas, "your people need you. You have the power to turn them to colonization instead of remaining here as aliens. Just remember that."

James did not bother to answer.

17

No End to Trouble

THE newly established white colonizers began regularly transporting small groups of black volunteers and the white agents appointed by the United States government to their African colony, Liberia. Almost all died of disease. Many of those who did survive were forced to flee from Liberia to Sierra Leone, for the African natives who had been friendly to Paul Cuffe were hostile to the new arrivals.

Therefore, James was shocked the day that Francis Devanney and Charles Levy, both employees in the sail loft, told him that they were leaving for Liberia.

Francis had once been a slave to the Speaker of the House of Representatives but had escaped. Knowing that a man of such character would be hard sought, James had purchased his freedom. Francis had paid James back within a year, although James, in his usual fashion, had released him immediately upon purchase. He was the leading apprentice in the loft and had worked closely with James in organizing the militia during the war of 1812.

Charles Levy was a young, fiery man whose freedom

James had purchased more recently. He had come to the sail loft looking for work, and James had hired him. A few weeks later, two white men came to claim him as a runaway. Reaching into his belt, Charles had pulled out a revolver and threatened to kill them. In the silence that fell over the watching workers, one of the men said in a soft southern drawl that displayed no fright at Levy's threat, "Mr. Forten, I would advise you to demand that this man return. It's against the law to harbor a fugitive."

Charles Levy's hand was shaking badly, and he held it steady with the other hand while easing toward the door.

"Are you his owner?" James asked the man who had spoken.

"Yes," answered the man. "Even though he is more trouble than he's worth."

"How much is he worth?" James asked.

"Oh, I could sell him I reckon for about the four hundred dollars I paid for him," the man answered. "Do you own this place?" he asked with interest.

James ignored his question. "I'll pay you four hundred dollars," he offered.

"It ain't hardly worth the trouble I've been through," the man answered. When James did not reply, the man looked at his partner. "What do you think?" he asked. The other man shrugged and made no comment. "I guess I'll take four hundred fifty dollars, cash." The man grinned. "He ain't nothing but trouble. You'll see."

"Thomas," James called to his nephew. "Go get Sidney." A few minutes later Sidney arrived and led the white men away to his office. After they left, all the men in the loft gathered around and shook Charles's hand.

"They knew I would have killed them," Charles kept repeating. "Mr. Forten didn't have to give them nothing. They knew I wasn't going back no how." When all the other employees had gone, Charles did approach James.

"Are you going to hold the money you gave them out of my pay every week?" he asked abruptly.

"Well, no," James answered, immediately annoyed. He handed Charles his emancipation papers. "You pay me back as you're able." He tried to smile. "With you working here, I'm sure I'll have no trouble getting my money back."

Charles had never made an effort to pay James or explain why, and James never asked. It always made him feel embarrassed to receive money from slaves he had emancipated anyway.

Now he sat studying Levy and Devanney. "Why are you going to Liberia?" he asked. His voice betrayed his anger in spite of himself.

Immediately, Charles flared up. "What do you mean 'why?'" he demanded angrily.

James observed tiredly that Charles was always angry, always demanding, always acting as if James were indebted to him. After a moment's reflection, James decided that he was glad Charles was going some-where—anywhere. He was weary of him.

"I never heard you mention going there before," James answered quietly.

"You know we'll never be able to share in the liberties of this country," cried Charles dramatically. "Our freedom is partial, and we have no hope that it will ever be otherwise."

In spite of his loud, dramatic voice, his words did not sound sincere. Instead, he sounded as if he were reciting words he had heard spoken by someone else. James turned to Francis and softened.

"What will you do there?" he asked.

"I'm not sure, sir," Francis answered. "I have been

asked to command a vessel to navigate the African coast and obtain supplies for the settlers. I believe that there will be many opportunities in a new colony."

"And I'm sure that you'll succeed in anything you do, Francis," James said with a smile. He liked Francis and realized that his reasons for being upset at the announcement of his departure were selfish ones. Francis was by far the brightest apprentice James had ever had in the loft and a dynamic force in the abolition movement. He depended on him so much that he didn't know how he would ever replace him.

Not long after their departure, James saw the trend of hate toward the black man grow even more pronounced. Law after law was passed to increase the oppression of all blacks, free and slave. Education was forbidden to slaves and to the southern blacks under penalty of death to both teacher and pupil. When the slave trade became illegal in 1808, many wealthy owners took to breeding slaves like livestock and later separating them from their families without regard to their humiliation and heartbreak. The kidnapping of young children spread terror through the northern cities as more and more children disappeared, never to be seen or heard from again.

In desperation, large numbers of slaves attempted escape and revolt, although the penalties, if they were caught, were grave indeed. The brilliant free black man, Denmark Vesey, almost succeeded in 1822 in carrying out an extensive slave revolt in Charleston, South Carolina, but he was betrayed in his plan to bring the city under black control.

In 1829 the white people of Cincinnati, Ohio, boldly decided to exterminate all the blacks of the city. The completely black neighborhoods were burned and hundreds of blacks killed. The rest were forced to flee, leaving all worldly possessions behind. Traveling day and night, many reached Canada safely.

That same year in Philadelphia, a white gang slipped into Bethel Church during one of Reverend Allen's services, threw cayenne pepper and salt into the stove, locked the doors on the congregation, and then cried out, "Fire! Fire!" In the panic that followed, dozens of people in the congregation were trampled to death. The gang was identified, but the legal authorities refused to take action against them.

James's heart went out to Richard Allen. He never forgot how the tears had run unashamedly down his friend's face afterward as the minister had asked, "What is there left for us?" He was a broken man, and it seemed that James could see him age before his eyes.

"Maybe if all the blacks in the country could just unite in a common goal, we could do something." James had spoken not even knowing himself what he meant. He had just wanted to arouse Richard from the unhealthy apathy that had overtaken him and set him working on a new project, a new plan of action for the betterment of the blacks such as he had been engaged in ever since James had known him.

Richard Allen responded and got in touch with a young man by the name of Hezekiah Grice, who had talked to him about gathering the black leaders of the nation at a mass meeting to decide whether the black man should leave or remain in the United States. An organizational task of this size could only be done effectively by a man of such great persuasion and respect as Richard Allen. He was equal to the task and called the first national convention of blacks in 1830. The white people of Philadelphia commented that the convention could accomplish nothing, for it had no legal power to back its action. Little did they realize the strength the blacks gained by unifying their efforts to combat oppression, not just locally but nationally.

From that time, the abolition movement became a nationwide movement. Composed of men with zeal, talent, and ability, the union poured such fire into the abolition cause that it was transferred from a protest against slavery to a demand for freedom. The knowledge of this success filled Richard Allen with pride, and death found him a few months later full of hope and confidence in the future of the black man in America.

18

The Merchant Prince

By 1830, James's wealth and bold efforts on behalf of his people had brought him respect from the whites as well as the blacks. He was fondly referred to as the "merchant prince."

When the first public school for blacks in Philadelphia opened, James finally gave up his volunteer teaching. With the time he now could call his own, he started a successful Infant School for children from two to five years of age. He felt the school was essential for the development of black children who had been deprived of a natural home life.

He was given an award by the Humane Society of Philadelphia when it was discovered that, during his lifetime, he was known to have rescued five white people from the Delaware.

In 1831, following the slave revolt led by Nat Turner—a bold young slave in Virginia—which resulted in the death of sixty white persons, the wrath of the white man was once again poured upon all blacks in America. During the summers of 1831 and 1832, white rioters attacked the black section of Philadelphia, mercilessly beating any blacks they could find. Churches were burned and homes torn down. The mayor finally had to appeal for special troops from the state, and they surrounded the area, forbidding the blacks to assemble in the city.

At this time a discriminatory bill to revoke Pennsylvania's resolutions that protected blacks against the Fugitive Slave Act was introduced in the state legislature. It had been thirty-nine years since James and Lucy had written their petition against the Fugitive Slave Act, but the same fear beset him again. He spent long hours researching the public records of Philadelphia to denounce the accusations of whites that blacks were a burden to taxpayers. He pointed out that the amount of taxes the blacks in Philadelphia paid far exceeded the amount of money Philadelphia spent on their poor. He stated that the blacks of Philadelphia owned over one hundred thousand dollars in real estate; that they had formed over fifty societies to meet the welfare needs of their own people, and that almost all blacks paid for the education of black children themselves.

"With our limited opportunity," James wrote, "we are far more useful citizens than whites who have ample opportunity."

James's petition was presented to the black leaders of Philadelphia, who endorsed it. The efforts to expose blacks to the Fugitive Slave Act and limit their emigration into Pennsylvania was defeated in the legislature.

James was disappointed when the first black newspaper, *Freedom's Journal,* folded in 1831. He felt that this was a tool the blacks needed to unite their efforts for abolition. He was, therefore, interested when a white abolitionist named William Lloyd Garrison wrote to ask him for financial support in starting a newspaper that would expose the hated system of slavery. Garrison hoped that

116

the newspaper would be effective in rallying people throughout the country to the abolitionist cause.

James donated money to Garrison, but when his requests for funds continued to increase, James discussed the matter with Sidney Brown, one of the few white men he felt he could talk with frankly. He asked the lawyer to investigate Garrison. Sidney could not help smiling as he reported to James.

"I don't know that you would like him personally," he said. "Garrison is an earnest young man who feels that slavery is wrong, but that the fate of black men rests in his hands alone. He thinks of them as lost sheep that he must save."

"Not another fatherly saint," James said.

"I'm afraid so," said Sidney. "He asked if you were a mulatto. I assured him that you were not."

They both laughed, and then Sidney went on more seriously. "Garrison's great weakness is that he has no respect for money. He spends it, not knowing where it's coming from. The causes are good, but his management is poor."

James was sixty-five years old. Although he was still involved in the abolition movement, he had begun leaving public affairs more and more in the hands of his two oldest sons, James, Jr., and Robert Bridges, and his son-in-law, Robert Purvis, who had married his daughter Harriet.

But as the *Liberator,* Garrison's newspaper, continued to struggle for existence, he himself came to call on James in Philadelphia.

"I am looking for Mr. Forten," a tall, thin, balding man stated when James opened his door one winter morning.

"I am he," James answered, slightly puzzled. He seldom had white visitors.

The man held out his hand. "I am William Lloyd
Garrison of the *Liberator.*" They shook hands, and James
invited him in. The Fortens were just preparing to eat
breakfast, and Charlotte, in her customary friendliness,
insisted he join them. James could not help being amused
by Garrison's surprise at his home.

118

"I had no idea that you lived so extravagantly," he told James when the two of them were alone. "I really did not expect this. You have such a refined family."

"What did you expect?" James asked.

"I really don't know," admitted Garrison frankly. "I always had the idea that Negroes lived much more simply."

"More like our forefathers in that distant hut three thousand miles away," put in James.

Catching the well-deserved sarcasm, Garrison laughed. James liked his frankness and sincerity.

"Mr. Forten," began Garrison, "we just must have additional support for the *Liberator*."

"The paper is supposed to be self-supporting," said James. "Where is the support of the white abolitionists? I hear their philosophies. I read their letters."

"The chief subscribers are Negro," Garrison admitted. "But we need your continued help to keep operating."

"I'm not that rich," said James quickly. "After all, I do want to leave an inheritance for my children."

"What better inheritance can you leave them than freedom?"

"I would like to leave them something more tangible also," James responded cynically.

"Do you mean that you will no longer support the *Liberator*?" Garrison seemed to grow very nervous. James noticed his worn clothes and his thin, tired look and realized the extreme sacrifice and suffering this young white man had undertaken in the name of abolition. In addition, the *Liberator* was accomplishing many things.

"No," he answered Garrison. "I don't mean that I won't support the *Liberator*. It's our greatest weapon."

Garrison smiled happily.

"Stay for a while," James suggested. "I will show you a

poem my daughter wrote."

Garrison agreed. The friendship that was established between the two men that first day was a lasting one, and Garrison became a frequent guest at the Forten home. Throughout the long years of the black struggle in America, the Forten family and Garrison remained close allies.

19

A Country Called Home

JAMES sat in his sail loft alone, inspecting some new rope that had been shipped in from Russia. The year was 1842, and he was seventy-six.

"Hello, Mr. Forten," someone greeted him.

James looked up, puzzled. The voice sounded vaguely familiar, but the years had dimmed his memory. It had been a long time since he had heard the voice of Francis Devanney, who had prospered so well in Liberia. He was high sheriff of the colony and very rich. Devanney had come by to see James briefly ten years before when he had testified in Washington on behalf of the colonizationists in an effort to get government funds to promote the growth of Liberia.

"Mr. Forten!" Another voice interrupted while James and Francis were still shaking hands. James had no trouble after twenty years recognizing the voice of Charles Levy.

"Hello, Charles," said James. "How are you doing?"

"Just as well as you are now," Charles said flippantly. "I am now doing just as well as you are."

James held his hand out to Charles, who pointedly

121

ignored it. "Thanks to you," he went on, "black people in America will never have the privilege of saying the same thing."

"Why did you come here?" James asked.

"I owe you some money," said Charles. "How much did I cost you? Four hundred or five hundred dollars?"

James didn't answer. Charles reached into his pocket and pulled several bills from a roll of money and threw them at James.

"Why are you angry with me?" he asked Charles.

"Because you are a traitor!" Charles yelled.

"Traitor?" James asked, puzzled.

Francis stood up. "Come on, Charles," he said. "He is just an old man now."

James motioned his hand for Francis to be quiet. He was interested. "Why do you call me that?" he asked.

"If it had not been for you, the blacks would not be in the condition they are in today. All over this country they are beaten, killed, sold, denied jobs and education."

"I am doing everything one human being can possibly do," said James.

"Yes. Your generosity is well known," spat out Levy. "You purchase a few dozen slaves. But there are thousands of others still in bondage. You help a few hundred escape through the Underground Railroad. But hundreds more do not make it. You give fifty or sixty jobs, but what about the uncounted others who will never be allowed to work? Who do you think you are? God?"

"You think I should have supported the colonization movement, I gather," said James.

"At least you should not have publicly opposed us. You should not have gathered the black people to crusade against us."

"You can only lead the people in the direction they

want to go," said James.

"I guess you live in the hope that someday your sons will be admitted to all the rights and privileges of citizenship in these United States?" Charles questioned James.

"I would hope so," said James.

"Well they won't," snapped Levy. "And you can bet your life that the black man hasn't been born yet that will see that day."

He turned and walked swiftly out of the sail loft. James didn't speak for a long time. Finally, he turned to Francis.

"Francis," he said, his voice sounding pained, "is Liberia all they claim it to be?"

Francis did not want to hurt James any more. "No," he answered.

James went on. "I know some blacks got rich there. I got rich here. But what about the masses, Francis? Are they really any better off?"

"Well," Francis said, "they do have pride."

"Pride is nothing without privilege," James retorted. "I hear of diseases, hostility of the Africans, and loneliness."

Francis made no further attempt to answer James.

"The black man was forced to come to America. Now he's being forced to leave America. His destiny remains in the hands of the white man. The choice for the black man is not between America or Africa; Liberia or liberty. As long as the white man is offering us our choices, it's like choosing between the devil and the sea. What we've got to decide is whether the white man will choose for us or whether we will choose for ourselves."

When James finished speaking, he suddenly felt very old. He walked Francis to the door and shook his hand. He then closed the door of the sail loft behind him for the last time.

He walked slowly toward home along the waterfront of the Delaware River, for he was very tired. He looked at the red sun sinking into the dark gray river and realized that his whole life was over. His shoulders ached and his eyes were heavy.

America was the land of his father, and his father's father, and his father's father before him. James rejoiced to know that he was dying in the only country that he could ever call home.

SUGGESTED READINGS

Aptheker, Herbert. *A Documentary History of the Negro People in the United States from Colonial Times to 1910.* New York: Citadel Press, 1969.

Barton, Rebecca Chalmers. *Witnesses for Freedom.* New York: Harper and Brothers, 1948.

Billington, Ray A. "James Forten: Forgotten Abolitionist." *Negro History Bulletin,* November 1949, p. 31.

Douty, Esther M. *Forten the Sailmaker: Pioneer Champion of Negro Rights.* Chicago: Rand McNally, 1968.

Hughes, Langston. *Famous Negro Heroes of America.* New York: Dodd Mead, 1958.

Hughes, Langston, and Meltzer, Milton. *Pictorial History of the Negro in America.* New York: Crown Publishers, 1968.

Kaiser, Ernest. *Historical Landmarks of Black America.* New York: Bellwether Publishing Company, 1971.

Ploski, Harry A. *Afro U.S.A.* New York: Bellwether Publishing Company, 1967.

Thomas, John L. *The Liberator, William Lloyd Garrison.* Boston: Little, Brown, 1963.

Wilkes, Laura Eliza. "Missing Pages in American History." In *The Negro Soldier, a Select Compilation.* New York: Negro Universities Press, 1970.

J
B   77-0114
For   Johnston, Brenda A.
          Between the devil and the sea

Appomattox Regional Library
Hopewell, Virginia 23860

1. Books may be kept two weeks and m
be renewed once for the same period, e
7 day books and magazines.

2. A fine is charged for each day a book is
not returned according to the above rule. No
book will be issued to any person incurring
such a fine until it has been paid.

3. All injuries to books beyond reasonable
wear and all losses shall be made good to the
satisfaction of the Librarian.

4. Each borrower is held responsible for all
books charged on his card and for all fines ac-
cruing on the same.